P9-DGC-058

Coaching Intermediate Synchronized Swimming Effectively

Kim E. Van Buskirk

Editor
Director of Educational Services
United States Synchronized Swimming

Contributing Authors

Kaaren Babb
Dawn Bean
Ross Bean
Christine Carver
Charlotte Davis
EmmaGene Edwards
Pamela Edwards
Gail Emery
Margret Swan Forbes

Peg Hogan
Virginia Jasontek
Kathy Kretschmer-Huss
Linda Lichter
Lillian MacKellar
Gail Pucci
Dorothy Sowers
Joanmarie Vanaski
JoAnn Wright

Avilee Goodwin
Illustrator

Human Kinetics Publishers, Inc.
Champaign, IL 61820

Library of Congress Cataloging-in-Publication Data

Van Buskirk, Kim E., 1952-
    Coaching intermediate synchronized swimming
effectively.

    Bibliography: p.
    1. Synchronized swimming. 2. Synchronized swimming--
Coaching. I. Title.
GV838.53.S95V36   1987   797.2'1   86-21343
ISBN 0-87322-086-2

Developmental Editor: Sue Wilmoth, PhD
Production Director: Ernie Noa
Assistant Production Director: Lezli Harris
Copy Editor: Janis Young
Assistant Editor: Kathy Kane
Typesetter: Theresa Bear
Text Layout: Denise Peters
Printed By: Versa Press
Artwork: Avilee Goodwin

ISBN: 0-87322-086-2

Copyright © 1987 by Human Kinetics Publishers, Inc.

All rights reserved. Except for use in a review, the reproduction or utilization of
this work in any form or by any electronic, mechanical, or other means, now
known or hereafter invented, including xerography, photocopying and recording,
and in any information retrieval system, is forbidden without the written permission of the publisher.

Printed in the United States of America

10 9 8 7 6 5 4 3 2 1

Human Kinetics Publishers, Inc.
Box 5076, Champaign, IL 61820

Acknowledgments

I am indebted to the contributing authors for their cooperation and timeliness in putting this book together. I appreciate the support of the staff at Human Kinetics Publishers, especially Dr. Rainer Martens, President, and Dr. Sue Wilmoth, Senior Editor. Because of Avilee Goodwin's sensitivity to synchronized swimming and artistic talent, the illustrations are lifelike and accurate.

My personal thanks go to the staff at United States Synchronized Swimming for their support, including Betty Watanabe, Brenda Scandaliato, Deena Pitman, Susan Lezotte, and Mike Minich. My gratitude goes to Nancy Wightman, Vice-President of Development, for her guidance and dedication to me. A very special thank-you is extended to Dawn Bean, President of Synchro-USA. She began my synchro career as my coach, helped me begin my club, guided me through the judging ratings, and supported and endorsed me while serving as the Director of Educational Services for United States Synchronized Swimming.

Kim E. Van Buskirk

U.S. Synchronized Swimming

Coaching Intermediate Synchronized Swimming Effectively serves as the official text of the U.S. Synchronized Swimming's National Coaches Certification Program. U.S. Synchronized Swimming, better known as Synchro-USA, is responsible for the education and training of athletes, coaches, judges, and officials on all levels of competition. This organization fields the championship teams that represent the U.S. in international competition, including the Olympic Games. Synchro-USA is recognized by the International Olympic Committee, the U.S. Olympic Committee, and FINA, the International Aquatic Federation.

Members of Synchro-USA receive a bimonthly newsletter which focuses on current issues and reports on the most current developments in the sport and in educational resources. Members also receive insurance benefits and more. For further information, contact the national headquarters in Indianapolis—Synchro-USA, 901 W. New York St., Indianapolis, IN 46223 (phone 317 633-2000).

Contents

Preface

Coaching Intermediate Synchronized Swimming Effectively is a continuation of *Coaching Synchronized Swimming Effectively,* which has been endorsed by the top age group coaches and is used by synchro teachers and coaches throughout the United States. The Coaching Certification Program uses both *Coaching Synchronized Swimming Effectively* and *Coaching Intermediate Synchronized Swimming Effectively,* and the books also comprise a major portion of the highly successful National Synchro-USA Camp curriculum.

Coaching Intermediate Synchronized Swimming Effectively provides an excellent tool to help coaches develop the skills of intermediate synchronized swimmers. The book is divided into two parts. Part 1 provides a discussion of the Intermediate Skills that are some of the most important components of figures. They are presented as Beginning Actions, Figure Movements (or Transitions), Ending Actions, Rotations, and Vertical Rotations. Once learned, these components can be applied to the execution of all figures that require that particular component. Coaches and swimmers can also combine components learned in Part 1 to create new hybrids for routine choreography.

Part 2 introduces the coach to putting the program together. The first chapter, on choreography, gives the reader a good idea of what is required and desired in a routine, including suggestions for both trio and team choreography. The next chapter, Conditioning, presents ideas for improving strength while sculling and includes a section on flexibility. The last chapter offers suggestions on how to plan a year-round program and how to organize the workouts. This chapter also offers some thoughts on age group programs and outlines factors to consider if the team is traveling for the first time.

Note: Participants in the United States Synchronized Swimming programs are predominantly female; hence *she* is used throughout the text in reference to the synchronized swimmer.

Part I: Intermediate Skills

The first part of this book presents skills that are appropriate for intermediate-level swimmers. It is a continuation of the logical progression established in *Coaching Synchronized Swimming Effectively,* which provided information on how to teach the necessary basic skills. No one complete figure is taught here. Instead, the authors have included the skills necessary to execute the various parts of the figures. Many of the techniques presented are used in more than one figure. For example, the Front Pike Pull Down is taught so that the swimmer can use it whenever she begins in a Front Layout and moves into a Front Pike position (as in a Front Walkover, a Subilarc, or a hybrid).

The chapters are arranged in a logical teaching progression for the intermediate-level coach and for Synchro-USA's Coaching Certification Program. All of the chapters in this section include the skills that intermediate level swimmers use most frequently. Some are repeated from the first book, with a more advanced technique for execution. Chapter 1 presents Beginning Actions; chapter 2 describes Figure Movements, or the middle parts of some figures; and chapter 3 teaches three of the more common Ending Actions. Chapter 4 introduces the Catalina and Reverse Catalina Rotations, and chapter 5 outlines the first Vertical Rotations the swimmer should attempt.

Chapter 1: Beginning Actions

Beginning actions in synchronized swimming are those skills used to initiate a figure action. The swimmer should practice these techniques until she has mastered them. When her performance of a beginning action becomes consistent, she can use it for every figure and/or hybrid that begins with that skill. Although many of the beginning actions are not presented here, the following are considered the most pertinent to the intermediate-level swimmer and coach:

- Bent Knee Dolphin
- Front Pike Pull Down
- Albatross Roll
- Straight Leg Archover
- Double Ballet Legs

Bent Knee Dolphin

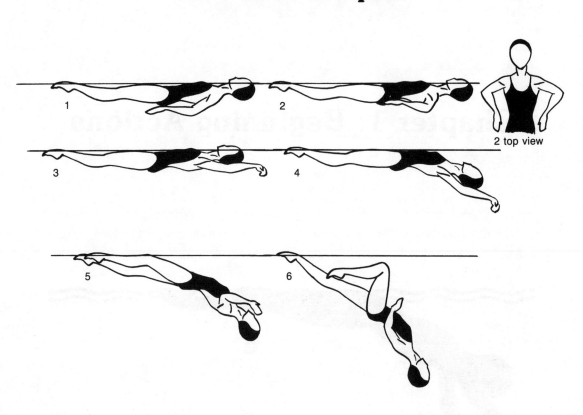

2 top view

Whenever a swimmer executes the beginning of a Bent Knee Dolphin she should use the technique explained here. A common problem swimmers experience with the Dolphin is that bending the knee on the descent causes the straight leg to submerge prematurely. The following method will help the swimmer perform a smooth beginning with control.

Method of Execution

To begin the Bent Knee Dolphin the swimmer assumes a Back Layout position. The position of the arms is optional. For any Dolphin, two arm positions are commonly used in the Back Layout. The swimmer may either place her arms by her side or extend them above her head in the water. If the arms are by the sides, the swimmer turns her palms downward and gently slides them along her body in a slicing manner with her elbows bending outward. The fingers will be toward the torso. The swimmer continues to move her hands and arms in this manner to the overhead position before moving her body headfirst with a Dolphin scull. This action should take about 8 to 12 counts. The swimmer then flexes her wrists to begin the Dolphin scull, causing the body to move headfirst. Lifting her chin very slightly, she presses her head and shoulders gently downward to enter the water. Lifting the feet keeps them from sinking underwater. The swimmer continues the Dolphin scull with wrists flexed and palms facing the top of the head as the body descends. She sculls her arms from overhead through an arc in front of and to the sides of her body until the hands reach the hips.

The swimmer should visualize a circle or clock with 12:00 o'clock at the surface, 3:00 o'clock at the side that she passes with her head pointed down, 6:00 o'clock closest to the bottom of the pool, and 9:00 o'clock at the side that she passes with her head pointed toward the surface. (See *Coaching Synchronized Swimming Effectively*, M.S. Forbes, 1984, p. 69 or 87.) The head enters the water at 12:00 o'clock. Before the knees submerge, one leg bends so that the foot moves along the inside of the other leg to begin the Bent Knee position. During the descent, the body continues to move through the arms. As she moves her body through her arms, the swimmer might think that she is sculling her arms to a position in front and to the sides of her body, as if her arms were reaching for the 12:00 o'clock position on the surface. The swimmer uses 8 to 12 sculls for this movement. Once the hands reach the hips or sides, the swimmer begins the Canoe scull and continues it until the head approaches the surface. Then the Standard scull is used.

As the swimmer assumes the Bent Knee, she draws the foot of the Bent Knee leg along the other leg smoothly and at a constant speed. The Bent Knee is assumed before the foot of the extended leg submerges. After the swimmer's head moves past 2:00 o'clock, she should feel as if she is lifting the extended leg out of the water to avoid pressing the foot inside the circumference of the circle. *Coaching Tip:* Think of lifting the toes of the extended foot out of the water to get this same effect.

Teaching Progression

On the Deck Have the Swimmers:

1. Assume a Back Layout position across a chair or diving board. After extending their arms overhead, they should flex their wrists sharply as they turn their palms outward to begin the Dolphin scull. Have a partner stand to the side and gently hold onto the swimmer's head for safety. The swimmers lean back and press their bodies through their arms as they move their arms in front and to the sides of their bodies. (This action must be simulated because it can only be done in the water.)

2. Observe a round object located near the pool (e.g., a clock or the drawing of a circle on a slate board or a large sheet of paper). Using stick figures, show the swimmers how they should be positioned in the Back Layout at 12:00 o'clock before performing the Bent Knee Dolphin. Explain where 2:00 o'clock is for the leg lift so that the foot moves along the circumference of the circle.

3. Practice the Bent Knee position. Instruct the swimmers to move the foot of their Bent Knee leg along the inside of the opposite leg until a Bent Knee is assumed at or above the knee of the opposite leg.

In the Water Have the Swimmers:

1. Review and practice the Dolphin as described in *Coaching Synchronized Swimming Effectively*, pages 69-71.

2. Perfect the beginning action of the Dolphin. Instruct the swimmers to move headfirst with Dolphin scull. They should press their heads and shoulders gently downward, moving their bodies through their arms.

3. Execute the beginning of a Bent Knee Dolphin. As the body descends, the swimmers should assume the Bent Knee position. For correct timing, they should begin the Bent Knee action as their knees reach 12:00 o'clock and complete the action before the foot of the extended leg submerges. The swimmers should aim for a deep spot on the wall behind them until the foot of their extended leg submerges. To keep from falling inside the circle when they assume the Bent Knee, the swimmers should press their rib cages and hips forward and concentrate on keeping the foot of the extended leg on the circle.

Common Errors	Corrections
• Movement toward the feet as the hands are brought over the head.	• Gently move the hands along the sides of the body. Turn the palms downwards or toward the body as if slicing them through the water. Or begin the action with the hands overhead in the Back Layout.
• Feet sinking when the Dolphin is begun.	• Do not arch the lower back. Press the feet upwards.
• Body does not move head-first.	• Flex the wrists sharply. Make sure the palms face toward the head.
• Suddenly forcing the head and shoulders downward, causing too steep an entrance into the water.	• Lift the chin and aim for a deeper point on the wall behind the head until the foot of the extended leg submerges.
• Arching the lower back too much as the Bent Knee is assumed, causing the body to pivot inside the circle.	• Loosen the arch in the lower back and aim for the wall behind the head.
• Bending the knee too soon so that the Bent Knee projects above the surface.	• Prior to the submergence of the knees, begin to move one foot along the inside of the other leg.
• Bending the knee too quickly, causing the body to straighten and drop inside the circumference of the circle.	• Bend the knee more slowly as the hips and foot of the extended leg are lifted to keep them on the circle. Allow the arc of the body to continue through the extended leg.
• Incorrect Bent Knee position.	• Keep the foot of the Bent Knee at or above the knee on the inside of the opposite leg.

*The term Dolphin scull has replaced the Reverse Torpedo scull.

Front Pike Pull Down

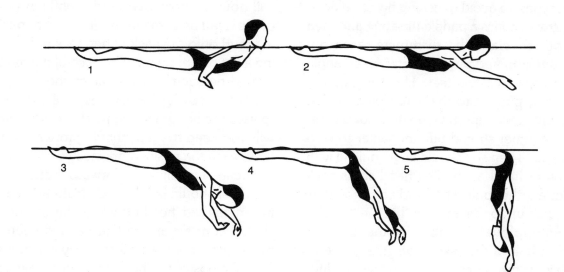

The Front Pike Pull Down is an important skill because the swimmer uses it every time she assumes a Pike position from the Front Layout. Some of the figures discussed in *Coaching Synchronized Swimming Effectively* require a Front Pike Pull Down as a part of their execution (e.g., Front Pike Somersault, p. 50; Jumpover, p. 52; and Front Walkover,

p. 85). That book simply recommends an All-igator scull or an adaptation of it to move the swimmer from the Front Layout into the Front Pike Surface Position. The intermediate-level swimmer can be taught the following more advanced way to execute this technique.

Method of Execution

The swimmer begins the Front Pike Pull Down in a Front Layout position, using a Canoe scull. The sculling is done primarily by the lower arm and wrist between the chest and hips. The armpits should be kept close to the body to minimize movement of the upper arms. Tell the swimmer to think of the torso as being tight and stretched. She should pull her buttocks and stomach into a spot 2 inches below the belly button to center her torso for a tightly balanced body line. This centering will enable the scull to be very relaxed to minimize any unnecessary movement. All movement should be controlled from within the center of the body, with this

center flowing all the way up the center line of the body. To obtain a breath, the swimmer extends her neck instead of the back or shoulders. Slowly placing her face in the water, she stops sculling and lets her arms float down and in front of her head approximately 12-15 inches beneath the surface. She depresses her head and shoulders below the surface and relaxes her hips to bend. Instruct the swimmer not to tuck her chin. Lead with the center point of the chest. The head should be kept in line with the shoulders. The upper back muscles (shoulder blade area) and the back of the neck muscles are used to press down on the back (as if a hand were placed on the upper back pressing it down.) The swimmer should stretch and flatten the upper chest to avoid hunching her shoulders. The arm action is a paddle (first one and then the other). Have the swimmers reach out with one arm and pull the water on an angle toward the face and feet. The palm should be facing parallel to the wall closest to the feet, with finger tips inward and elbows bent. The swimmer should pull the water toward the head. Then she should begin pulling with the other hand as the first hand slices back up for another pull. The head and shoulders will catch up to the arms so that the paddles will end up over the crown of the head for the last half of the pike down. As one arm is pulling, the other is slicing or recovering, as if the swimmer were climbing a rope. She should make large, slow smooth pulls. As the body reaches a 45-degree angle, the hands should rotate to keep the palms facing the feet. This action will help the swimmer keep pulling the water toward her feet. The pulls will now be more over and slightly in back of the head and smaller (as if she were packing mud onto the back of her neck or knocking a hat off her head). The pitch of the hands should be such that it enables the body to continue moving forward as well as down toward the bottom of the pool. Correct pitch will also keep the hips moving forward until they reach the position originally occupied by the head. To help keep forward motion, the swimmer should feel as if her thighs are pressing in toward her buttocks. The swimmer should contract and pull in the abdomen to make sure it is used all the way down into the Pike position. The Front Pike is reached at the same time the hips reach the starting point of the head. At this point, the hands should still be over the head.

Teaching Progression

On the Deck Have the Swimmers:

1. Stand and practice the paddling action with the arms as they bend at a right angle at the waist, keeping the back flat.

2. Get a feel for a good Pike position while sitting on the deck.

In the Water Have the Swimmers:

1. Use the side of the pool to practice the Front Pike position illustrated.

2. Use a flotation device to support their feet while they practice the paddling action with their arms, pulling down into a Pike position.

3. Have a partner mark with her hand the starting position of the swimmer's head. Instruct the swimmer to practice the paddling action down to the Pike position until her buttocks touch the partner's hand.

4. Perform the entire skill using the paddling action of the hands.

Common Errors	**Corrections**
• Feet dropping below the surface as the Pike begins.	• Lead with the chest. Press up on the heels and tighten the muscles in the front of the legs.
• Buttocks popping out of the water as the Pike begins.	• Do not begin the Pike until forward movement starts. Make sure the arm pull is deep enough so that the body pikes from the hips, not from the waist. Push back on the shoulders and lead with the chest.
• Head dropping and shoulders rounding.	• Push back on the shoulders and keep the head in line with the trunk. Lead with the chest.
• Failure to move forward so that the hips move to a position over the head.	• Stretch into the pull-down. While learning, use a small Breast Stroke before starting the downward movement. Rotate the palms of the hands so they are facing the feet in order to keep pulling the water toward the feet. Keep pulling the stomach into the backbone. Do not hyperextend the chest or arch the head and shoulders.
• Overpiking.	• Push back on the shoulders and head. Lead with the chest. Try to arch the back slightly while piking.

Albatross Roll

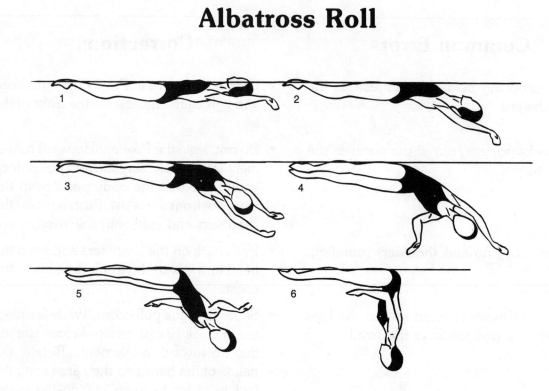

The Albatross Roll is used specifically in the Albatross figures. Once mastered, however, it also can be used in more creative and unique hybrid beginnings.

Method of Execution

The swimmer begins this action with the Dolphin scull as described in *Coaching Synchronized Swimming Effectively*, pages 69-71, for a Dolphin. After approximately the third outward scull, the head is gently tipped back to begin submergence of the head and shoulders. The swimmer travels headfirst while submerging her head, neck, shoulders, and upper chest. When the ribcage is submerged about halfway, she begins rolling toward the left by dropping her left shoulder and stretching the right side of her body. She should feel as if her hips are leading the roll. The left arm drops toward the bottom of the pool, maintaining the Dolphin scull with the emphasis on the inward scull. The right arm reaches and stretches over the head in a Dolphin scull with the emphasis on the out-

ward scull. The arch in the hips should be maintained during the first half of the roll. At the midpoint of the roll, when the body is facing the side wall, the left arm should be gradually sculled down toward the hips while it keeps pulling the body headfirst to continue the head-first flow. The right arm is still doing a Dolphin scull during this transition. The swimmer should begin slowly piking in the hips by tightening the stomach muscles, being careful to keep the legs stationary (not moving from side to side). As she completes the roll onto the stomach, she turns her left hand over into a Support scull under the thighs and gradually cuts her right arm down to join the left in Support scull. There should be enough forward movement so that the hips end up where the head began at the finish of the roll. This action is really just a rotation of the shoulders and hips, while keeping the legs turning on their axis. Constant pressure of the legs toward the surface of the water during the entire sequence will help stabilize the swimmer.

Teaching Progression

On the Deck Have the Swimmers:

1. Stand and practice the Dolphin sculling action of the hands.

2. Stand with a partner's hands placed on the swimmer's shoulders for support. The swimmers arch their backs and then turn and bend at the waist into a 90-degree angle while using the described arm action and timing.

In the Water Have the Swimmers:

1. Practice the beginning of the Dolphin. They should stop the movement when the roll begins—about the midpoint of the ribcage.

2. Begin rolling into a Pike position when the chest is halfway submerged as described above in the Method of Execution.

3. Begin in a Back Layout position perpendicular to the side of the pool. The swimmer should extend the hands overhead—about 4 to 6 inches from the wall—for the Dolphin scull. They should scull toward the wall, rolling over into the Pike position. The buttocks, back, shoulders, and back of the head should line up against the wall. Have the swimmers use a partner to support and help roll the legs.

4. Practice the skills away from the wall.

Common Errors

- No head-first movement at the beginning.

- Foot-first movement into the Front Pike.

- Sideways movement of the legs during the roll.

- Feet sink during the roll.

Corrections

- Flex wrists and keep the pulling action of the Dolphin scull constant.

- As the left arm drops down, continue Dolphin scull with both hands to pull the buttocks over the head.

- At the beginning of the roll, concentrate on keeping the feet stationary. Practice on the wall or with a partner holding the feet stationary.

  During the roll, lead with the hips and maintain stretch in the right side. Do not pike too soon or too quickly; it will cause the feet to swing.

- At the beginning, press the backs of the legs toward the surface. After the body begins to roll, press the outside of the left leg toward the surface. Toward the end of the roll, press the front of the legs toward the surface.

Straight Leg Archover (Hightower or Straight Leg Swordfish)

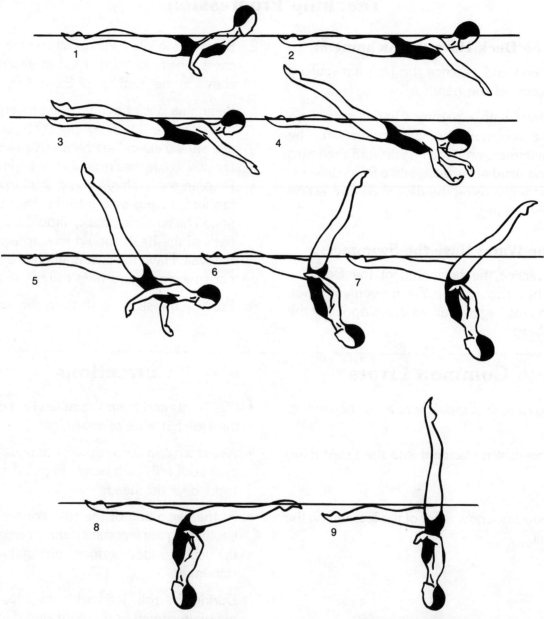

Straight Leg Archover into
Straight Leg Swordfish 6, 7, 8

Straight Leg Archover into
Hightower 6, 7, 9

This beginning action will be used in the Straight Leg Swordfish and the Hightower figures—both of which are found in intermediate through advanced levels of competition. Because the initial movement is an arching over, this action is unique and lends itself to a creative hybrid when found in rou-

tine choreography. The explanation here of the Straight Leg Archover is followed by a description of how to finish into the Splits position for a Straight Leg Swordfish and how to finish into the correct position for the Hightower.

Method of Execution

The swimmer begins this skill in a Front Layout position. One leg is lifted in an arc over the surface of the water. The following information describes how to lift the right leg; reverse the procedure for the opposite leg.

In the Front Layout, the swimmer should scull primarily with lower arm and wrist action between the chest and hips, holding the armpits close to the body to minimize arm movement. Tell them to think of the body being tight, stretched, and centered. The buttocks and stomach should be pulled into a spot 2 inches below the belly button. Neck extension action (no shoulders or back) is used to take a breath. The swimmer then stops sculling and hangs her arms loosely below the shoulders and extended out in front of the body on a 45-degree angle. The chest and chin are depressed toward the bottom of the pool by shortening the front side of the body and contracting the stomach muscles. Tell the swimmers they should feel as if someone's hand is pressing down on their upper back. The heel is lifted off the surface by tightening the buttocks and the back of the upper thigh and dropping the hips slightly toward the bottom. The swimmer should keep using the front side of the thigh to press the leg up. The arm action begins after the heel lifts slightly above the surface. The beginning pulls are actually paddles, one hand and then the other. (This will be referred to as the Paddle scull.) The swimmer pulls water on a diagonal angle toward her chest and feet with finger tips pointed inward and the elbows outward, in an effort to pull the body slightly headfirst. This action will help the leg go up and over and prevent foot-first movement. The paddles are small at first (two to three on each hand). The head and shoulders will catch up with the hands. Then about three larger pulls are made by reaching the hands down closer and closer to the thighs, which keeps the arms and body moving down toward the bottom

of the pool at the same pace. The buoyancy of the swimmer will dictate how soon the hands must move down under the hips and thighs (the less buoyant, the sooner). As the arm action begins, the swimmer keeps pressing the chest toward the bottom of the pool. The sides of the torso and hips are kept tight to prevent the leg from "wagging" from side to side, as the paddling action sometimes causes it to do. The hips must arch very hard to prevent any piking at the beginning. The hands should change to a Support scull as soon as possible. For most swimmers, this will occur when the leg reaches the 12:00 o'clock position.

Straight Leg Swordfish

The hips must press forward very hard during the second half of the arc. The hands remain in Support scull from 12:00 o'clock to the Split position. The swimmer begins to flatten her back by pulling her stomach into the small of the back during the second half of the arc. The arch in the Split position should only be in the hips and lower back. The upper back and head are vertical. Tell the swimmers they should feel as if their front leg is being pulled forward, while being careful to keep their hips as square as possible. They should not rest in the Split position. Have them use a Support scull that is strong enough to keep the crotch and the backs of the legs at the surface.

Hightower Position

The leg stops moving after it has passed the vertical and is in a position in which the foot is directly over the head. The swimmer then straightens her back by contracting her stomach muscles to pull the horizontal leg and hips into the tailbone, then squeezing the belly button into the small of the back, and "shortening" the horizontal leg to achieve a Vertical. The vertical leg moves into alignment with the torso. While continuing a Support scull, the hands will move from slightly behind the hips to slightly in front during the move to vertical alignment. The foot of the horizontal leg is pressed slightly toward the bottom of the pool so that the leg becomes parallel to the surface. During the straightening of the torso, the level of the hips should rise imperceptibly, depending on their depth in the arched position. A full torso and leg stretch is necessary for better extension, height, and control as the swimmer reaches the Crane position.

Teaching Progression

On the Deck Have the Swimmers:

1. Lie on their stomachs and practice lifting both ankles off the floor and then continue to raise one leg higher. Use the buttocks and thigh muscles to lift the legs.

2. In the same position, have a partner pull the leg up for full stretch and flexibility. Then instruct the partner to resist lifting and lowering one leg to build strength. To prevent injury, make sure the swimmer signals to her partner when to stop lifting the leg.

In the Water Have the Swimmers:

1. In a Front Layout position, use the Paddle scull described for the beginning of the Straight Leg Swordfish to travel down the pool head first.

2. Practice the same Paddle scull in the Front Layout moving down the pool. Keep the knees straight. Lift one foot off the surface of the water by squeezing the buttock and tightening the back of the thigh and pressing up with the front of the thigh.

3. Rest the front of the horizontal foot on the gutter. Have a partner press down on the upper back with one hand as she lifts the other leg with the other hand in an arc over the surface. The swimmer should concentrate on the proper hand and body technique described above.

4. Same as Number 3 above without a partner.

5. Practice the same actions away from the wall with and without a partner.

Common Errors	**Corrections**
• Stressing and using too much arm action at the beginning.	• Use more abdominal and chest contraction and hip arch. Contract the back of the thigh to begin the leg lift.
• Piking at beginning.	• Have a partner press down on the buttocks and lift up on the leg. Tighten the buttocks and press the hips forward.
• Body travels foot-first during the lift.	• Be sure beginning paddles are pulls toward the chest, pulling the body head-first. Loosen the arch in the upper back and neck, and depress the head and shoulders toward the bottom as if someone were pressing down on the back. Pull the horizontal leg into the hips (shorten it).
• Body travels head-first at the beginning.	• Make the pulling actions with the hands more gentle.
• Wagging of the lifting leg from side to side.	• Keep the muscles in the waist area tight and the arms in line with the shoulders.
• Hips sink after leg lifts off the surface.	• Move hands down under the hips sooner and hold the horizontal leg at the surface.
• Horizontal leg sinks during initial lift of the first leg.	• Keep pressing the front of the thigh of the horizontal leg toward the surface. Loosen the arch in the upper back and neck, and depress the head and shoulders. (For the Straight Leg Swordfish do not try to achieve a wide Split too quickly. Think only of the top leg moving into splits. It takes longer for the body to travel down under the hips than for the leg to move over the hips, so slow the leg action down.)
• Low height and hips sinking.	• Prevent the hands from paddling up over the head. Keep them near the surface as they are transferred to Support scull.
• Foot-first travel on the second half of the arc for the Straight Leg Swordfish.	• Constantly change the pitch of the hands as the body moves down, keeping palms flat to the bottom during Support scull.

Double Ballet Legs

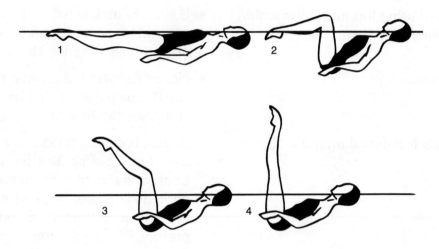

This skill is used in all of the Double Ballet Legs figures listed in Group 1 of the Official Synchro-USA Rulebook. By the time swimmers are taught this skill, they should be strong enough to hold the Double Ballet Legs for a moment before returning to the Back Layout or collapsing.

Method of Execution

The swimmer starts in a Back Layout position using a stationary Standard scull. Both legs are drawn up to a Tub position until the thighs are perpendicular to the surface. From this position, the swimmer lifts both bent legs until they are fully extended vertically from the hips. The thighs should remain still while the lower legs are lifted. The movement from the Back Layout to the Bent Knee and from the Bent Knee to the vertical position of the legs should be slow, controlled, and continuous. The swimmer should pause briefly in the Bent Knee position. *Coaching tip*: Tell the swimmers to think about lifting the toes to straighten the legs; this makes the actual execution seem easier.

Teaching Progression

On the Deck Have the Swimmers:

1. Assume a Back Layout position and lift the heels just off the floor. From this position, they should draw the knees toward the chest to the Tub position. After checking to make sure the thighs are perpendicular to the floor, they should lift the lower legs to the Double Ballet Legs position. The swimmers should concentrate on moving evenly from one position to the next so that the head and shoulders are horizontal to the surface and remain that way.

In the Water Have the Swimmers:

1. Assume a Back Layout with their feet on the gutter. Practice drawing the legs from the gutter to the Tub position, making sure that the legs move toward the body. Watch that the swimmers do not scull into the wall or away from it. Have them look toward the ceiling, keeping the mouth and chin dry. The shoulders should be down and flat. Be especially careful that their thighs are perpendicular to the surface in the Tub position.

2. Assume a Tub position with both feet resting on the gutter, and practice lifting to the Double Ballet Legs position. Stress "thinking the scull." At the beginning of the lift, the sculling action is moderate. As the legs move into the air, the scull increases in speed and moves deeper in the water. The shoulders and head remain back as in the Tub position. Tell the swimmers to think of expanding the ribcage out to the side and breathing from the diaphragm.

3. Practice numbers one and two away from the gutter.

4. Practice numbers one and two in progression as done in the figure.

Common Errors

- Top of the feet go underwater when they are drawn into the Tub position.

- Bending the legs too far or not far enough so that the thighs are not perpendicular.

- Head pulls forward so swimmer is looking at her legs.

- Shoulders are rounded and pulled toward legs.

- Scull sloshes on the lift.

- Failure to lock the knees in the Double Ballet Legs position.

- Face goes underwater in the Double Ballet Legs vertical position.

Corrections

- Lift the top of the ankles on the draw.

- Have another swimmer hold a short pole or yardstick or a flutter board on edge at the position where the thighs will be perpendicular. The swimmer will feel the correct perpendicular position when she touches the object.

- Focus eyes on the ceiling pushing the chin forward as a bird would peck.

- Use the stomach muscles and shins to lift legs. Keep arms in proper position for Standard scull.

- Make sure hands move deeper as legs go higher. Correct arms if they move rigidly and straighten them on the lifting action. Make sure the hands are not overturned on the inward scull.

- Do stretching exercises for the legs daily.

- Practice increasing the scull as the legs move into the air. Do widths and then lengths of Double Ballet Legs carry to develop the strength necessary to hold this position.

Chapter 2: Figure Movements/Transitions

The figure movement, or transition, comes between the beginning and ending action of a figure. This portion of the figure often distinguishes it from others that might begin and/or end similarly. Many of the more complex figures may include more than one of these movements, or transitions. Coaches and swimmers can benefit greatly from a thorough understanding of how to execute each individual skill correctly. Thinking of a whole figure in its entirety can be overwhelming even after it has been learned. The figure becomes less difficult to perform if the swimmer and coach break it down into its parts—beginning, middle (figure movements, or transitions), and ending—and execute it accordingly. Remember to work on one action at a time, waiting until the swimmer can execute it before moving on to the next phase of the figure.

Like beginning actions, figure movements—once they have been mastered—should be applied to every part of a figure or hybrid that includes that skill. Not all figure movements, or transitions, are presented here. Included are those techniques considered to be the most important to intermediate-level swimmers and coaches: Ballet Leg Submarine; Single and Double Ballet Leg Roll Actions; Eiffel Tower Layover; Elevator Action; Swordasub Action; Roll-Lift Action; Bent Knee Join to Vertical; and the Crane Join to Vertical.

Ballet Leg Submarine

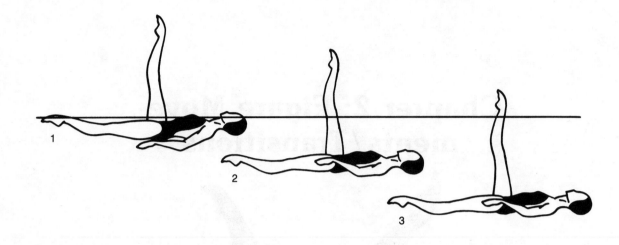

This skill is an important basic action because it is used in figures executed in intermediate levels of competition. The Ballet Leg Submarine precedes the roll action taught later in this chapter.

Method of Execution

From a strongly supported Ballet Leg, the swimmer should squeeze the buttocks and thigh of the horizontal leg, press her shoulder blades back and together, stretch her upper chest and gently exhale at least half of her air. (Depending on the buoyancy of the swimmer, more air may have to be exhaled.) Simultaneously, the sculling action should be relaxed while the shoulders, head, and horizontal leg are pressed toward the bottom of the pool. This gives the swimmer the feeling of trying to lift the hip area as the rest of the body and the horizontal leg are sinking. As the body begins to sink, the swimmer presses up on the Ballet Leg with the buttocks. She puts pressure on the chest and face to press the torso under. The body remains tight and locked in position during the sink. Just before she reaches the desired level (at about mid-calf), the swimmer increases the sculling tempo and power to ease into the desired submarine level (just above the ankle bone).

Teaching Progression

On the Deck Have the Swimmers:

1. Practice the Ballet Leg position lying flat to get the feeling of the horizontal locked position.

In the Water Have the Swimmers:

1. Lie on the bottom of the shallow end of the pool in a Ballet Leg position. Two partners should help the swimmer stay on

the bottom and not float toward the surface. One partner should press on the shoulders and the other on the horizontal leg to help cause an even sink. From the bottom, the swimmer should scull to the surface in the Ballet Leg position.

Common Errors	Corrections
• The horizontal leg floats up as the body submerges.	• Maintain full body extension and press down on the heel. In the submerged position, when the horizontal leg is in line with the body and parallel to the surface, the swimmer will feel as though the leg is much lower than the head.
• The head moves forward and the shoulders round.	• Keep the head in line with the body and press the shoulders back.
• Not enough air exhaled.	• Be sure to blow out air before attempting to sink.
• Traveling during the submergence.	• Keep pitch of the hands flat to the bottom.
• Abrupt, uncontrolled stop at ankle level.	• Begin increasing the scull tempo and power before reaching the desired level in order to ease into that level. Do not grab or pull at the water to stop.

Single Ballet Leg Roll Action

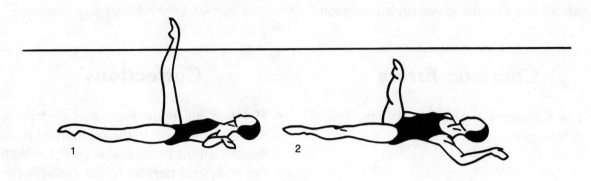

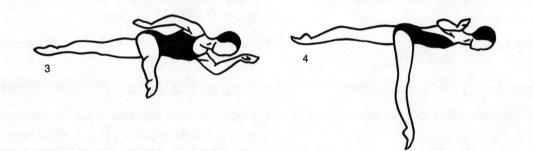

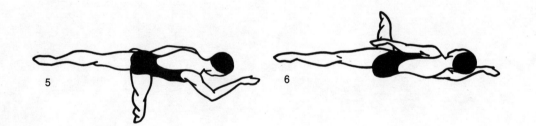

This action is used for the Single Ballet Leg Roll, and for the Sub-Crane. The Sub-Crane is done in junior national through international figure competitions. Proper execution of the roll will help the swimmer to align her body in the technically correct position necessary for achieving good scores. The following methods have been effective in teaching swimmers this skill.

Method of Execution

This action begins from the Ballet Leg Submarine position (see *Coaching Synchronized Swimming Effectively*, p. 11, 96-97.) The swimmer holds this position, moving the Ballet Leg around the body in a circle. She points the leg first to the side wall across the non-Ballet Leg, then to the bottom of the pool, then to the other side wall, and finally returns to the starting position. The torso, head, and non-Ballet Leg should remain horizontal and parallel to the surface of the water throughout. The Ballet Leg should remain perpendicular to the body. The movement should be slow, controlled, and continuous.

From the Ballet Leg position, the descent should be slow with head and feet descending at the same rate. It is preferable to sink while maintaining the sculling action at the hips instead of throwing the hands over the head. Relax the sculling and let the weight of the leg start the descent. The descent continues until the water level is near the ankle with the hands sculling near the hips to stabilize the position. To begin the roll to the left, place the left hand at the shoulder level (Totem position) while the right continues sculling at the hip. As the "T" position is reached with the toe pointed toward the bottom, the left hand moves under the chest to join the right hand with the fingertips of both hands pointed toward the bottom. As the roll continues, the right hand is brought to shoulder level Totem position while the left continues to scull at the hip/stomach level. When the three-quarter point of the roll is reached, both hands resume sculling at the hip level for the rise to the surface. The foot should break the surface at the same level from which the roll began. The rise follows the description of the Single Ballet Leg Submarine.

Teaching Progression

On the Deck Have the Swimmers:

1. Assume a right Ballet Leg position. (This makes it easier to teach. Switch for the left leg.) Practice lowering the Ballet Leg to the left side wall across the non-Ballet Leg. After the leg touches the floor, check for the 90-degree angle on the Ballet Leg at the hips. The Ballet Leg should be lying on its side. Then the knee should be bent to return to the Ballet Leg position. Repeat several times.

2. Assume the side Ballet Leg position on the right side of the body. Practice lifting and rolling from this position to the Ballet Leg position. Check the position, and have the swimmers bend their knee and roll back to the same side position. Repeat several times.

In the Water Have the Swimmers:

1. Repeat the deck drills on the surface of the water with one foot on the pool gutter.

2. In shallow water, assume a submerged right Ballet Leg position with the horizontal non-Ballet Leg, torso, and head on the bottom of the pool. At this water level, swimmers should practice the roll they did on the deck in Number 1 above.

3. Assume a side Ballet Leg position to the left on the surface of the water. The foot of the non-Ballet Leg should be resting on the gutter. Have the swimmers practice rolling toward the bottom and then to the other side, making sure that their hips, back, and head remain flat on the surface. Repeat several times.

4. Assume a submerged right Ballet Leg position in deep water with the *left* foot touching the wall and practice the complete roll action.

5. Practice the Single Ballet Leg Roll Action away from the wall.

Common Errors	Corrections
• Ballet Leg falls toward the face in the submerged position.	• Lock the 90-degree pike at the hip and push the back of the Ballet Leg knee away.
• Ballet Leg falls toward the face as the roll is executed.	• Emphasize Number 1 above. Return to the wall to get the proper feel of the perpendicular position.
• Shoulders are rounded, and head is pulled toward legs during the roll.	• Check arms to make sure they have not straightened. Make sure head and shoulders are pressed back and flat. Return to the shallow end and get the feeling of the submerged position with the head and shoulders on the bottom of the pool.
• As the torso approaches the halfway point (Ballet Leg pointing down), it begins to float up.	• Press the shoulders back to stretch the spine. Exhale a small amount of air. Shorten the sweeps of the scull.
• As the body approaches the halfway point, it begins to drop deeper in the water.	• When doing the short sweeps of the scull, make sure the palms are not pressing toward the surface or "patting" the water.
• At the halfway point, the swimmer ends up standing on her head.	• Return to the wall and practice the feeling of the legs pulling the body around. Imagine the toes of the Ballet Leg are touching the numbers of a clock. Imagine the foot of the non-Ballet Leg is locked in a vice grip.

Double Ballet Leg Roll Action

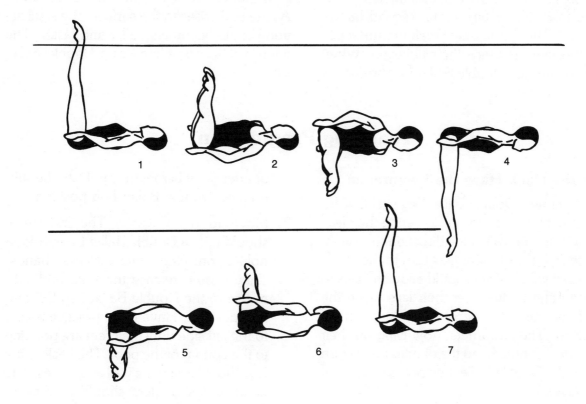

This action is used only for the Double Ballet Leg Roll. Although it is generally not found in the required figure competitions, the Double Ballet Leg Roll is used as an optional in figure competition by developing swimmers. The teaching progressions are similar to those for the Single Ballet Leg Roll.

Method of Execution

The action begins from the Double Ballet Leg Submarine position. The swimmer holds this position as she moves her legs around the body in a vertical circle, pointing first to the side wall, next to the bottom of the pool, then to the other side wall, and finally returning to the starting position. The torso and head should remain horizontal and the legs perpendicular to the body throughout. The movement should be slow, controlled, and continuous.

To begin the descent, sink with the hands at the hips, pressing back on the shoulders and neck as the outward scull is widened. Use slow, wide sculls as the air in the chest is slowly exhaled. Continue the descent until the water level is near the ankles, then stabilize the position by firming and shortening the scull. Drop the left shoulder as the head turns toward the left to begin the roll action. Use the weight of the legs moving left to help the body turn. The hands remain sculling at the hips with the right slightly in front of the hip on the first half of the roll, and the left slightly in front of the hip on the second half of the roll. The feet should break the surface in the position in which the roll began. When the submerged Double Ballet Leg position is reached, stabilize the action with a flat scull with the hands slightly above the hip level. As the body rises to the surface, the scull action should become smaller and faster. The figure will be completed as a Double Ballet Leg.

Teaching Progression

On the Deck Have the Swimmers:

1. Assume a Double Ballet Leg position. Instruct them to practice lowering their legs to the side wall in the direction they want to roll. (Most swimmers turn to the left or clockwise.) They should allow the legs to pull the body. After their legs touch the floor, check for the 90-degree angle at the hips. The swimmers, now lying on their sides, should bend their knees and return to the Double Ballet Leg position. Repeat several times.

2. Assume the side position on the right side. Practice lifting and rolling from this position to the Double Ballet Leg position. Check the position, and instruct them to bend the knees and roll to the same side position. Repeat several times.

In the Water Have the Swimmers:

1. Assume a Double Ballet Leg submerged position in shallow water. The back of the legs should touch the wall and the head and back should be on the bottom of the pool. Have the swimmers practice rolling to the left side wall as they did on the deck in Number 1 above.

2. Practice rolling in shallow water from the right side wall to Double Ballet Leg submerged position as they did on the deck in Number 2 above. Emphasize that the back of the legs should touch the wall throughout the roll. Check that the swimmers are looking at the side wall at the quarter point before they roll into the submerged Double Ballet Leg position.

3. Move to deep water. The swimmers should take a Double Ballet Leg position holding onto the gutter with their hands. They should release the hold and submerge to the Double Ballet Leg Submarine position. Have them practice rolling to the left side until their feet are pointing to the bottom of the pool. The back of the legs should touch the wall at all times. The head and shoulders should stay back. Make sure that the swimmers see the wall and then the bottom. Have them tuck and return to the surface. Repeat several times.

4. Assume the ending position from the last drill, legs touching the wall, feet pointing down to the bottom of the pool. Have them practice rolling up to the Double Ballet Leg Submarine position, keeping the legs in contact with the wall at all times. The head and shoulders should stay back. Make sure the swimmers see the bottom, the side wall, and then the surface. Then they should tuck and return to the surface. Repeat several times.

5. Practice combining the two drills from Number 3 and 4 so that a full circle is executed.

6. Return to shallow water and practice the first two shallow water drills away from the wall.

7. Return to deep water and practice the

deep water drills (Number 3 and Number 4) away from the wall. Check the water line at the start and finish after the full roll has been completed. Stress that the water line should be at the same point on the leg between the ankle and knee at both the start and finish. As the feet approach pointing to the bottom, stress that the shoulders should be pressed back and flat. At this point, the scull should become short sweeps until the feet point to the right side wall.

Common Errors	Corrections
• Legs fall toward the face in the vertical position of the Double Ballet Leg Submarine.	• Lock the 90-degree pike at the hips and push the back of the knees away.
• Legs fall toward the face as the roll is executed.	• Emphasize Number 1 above. Return to the wall to get the proper feel of the perpendicular position.
• Shoulders are rounded and head is pulled toward legs during the roll.	• Check arms to make sure they have not straightened. Make sure head and shoulders are pressed back and flat. Return to shallow end and get the feeling of the submerged position with the head and shoulders on the bottom of the pool.
• The torso begins to float as it approaches the halfway point.	• Press the shoulders back to stretch the spine. Exhale a small amount of air. Shorten the sweeps of the scull.
• As the body approaches the halfway point, it begins to drop deeper in the water.	• When doing the short sweeps of the scull, make sure the palms are not pressing toward the surface, or "patting" the water.
• At the halfway point, the swimmer ends up standing on her head.	• Return to the wall and practice the feeling of the legs pulling the body around. Imagine the feet touching the numbers of a clock rather than pressing into the turn.

Eiffel Tower Layover

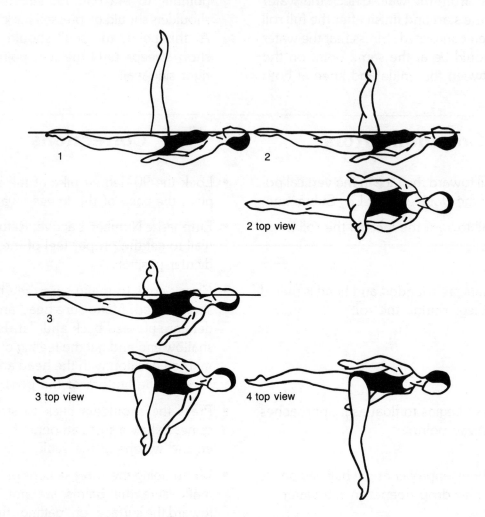

This action is used from a Ballet Leg in the Eiffel Tower and Eiffel Walk figures. It is a good skill for the intermediate swimmer to master and for the more advanced swimmer to review. Like many of the movements presented in this chapter, this skill can be used creatively to develop a new hybrid for routine choreography.

Method of Execution

The swimmer assumes a right Ballet Leg. To lay the Ballet Leg across the body to the surface of the water, she should begin pressing in on the inside of the extended leg and tighten the muscles on both sides of the leg to control the speed at which it moves. She then presses back on her right shoulder, rolling the torso as little as possible. Twisting in her waist and rolling her hips, she tightens and presses up on her left buttock to keep the hips from sinking. Just after the leg begins moving across, she should begin rolling her head to the left. During the last half of the Layover, the left hand reaches out away from the body to support the weight of the leg as it comes closer to the surface. To keep the head horizontal, it should feel as though the left ear is connected to the left shoulder during the last part of the roll. The head should roll as far to the side as possible without allowing the mouth to go into the water. To control the leg's entrance into the water the swimmer should delay the foot from entering the water just before it touches the sur-

face. The leg movement is slowed just above the surface by tightening the right outer thigh and buttock muscles. The left leg rolls over toward the outside of the leg at the same speed as the head. The left leg must be kept in the same horizontal and vertical planes as it was in the extended Ballet Leg position (no sinking or sideways movement).

Teaching Progression

On the Deck Have the Swimmers:

1. Perform the Ballet Leg. They should lock in this position and rotate to the side opposite the vertical leg. Swimmers should concentrate on maintaining a right angle between the legs and keeping the body fully extended and aligned.

In the Water Have the Swimmers:

1. Perform a Ballet Leg with horizontal leg supported on the pool gutter. The swimmers should rotate into the Eiffel position, using the techniques described in the Method of Execution.

2. Practice the skill away from the side of the pool.

Common Errors

- Horizontal leg sinks during the Layover.

- Hunching and rounding shoulders.

- Piking in the hips.

- Head protrudes out of the water.

- Right shoulder rolls over, causing right hand sculls to become too shallow and leg to plop uncontrolled in the water.

Corrections

- Press up toward the surface with the muscles on the inside of the horizontal leg. As the leg rolls over about halfway, press up toward the surface with the muscles on the outside of the horizontal leg.

- Press shoulders back and down. Stretch the torso.

- Tighten and squeeze the left buttock muscles and press hips forward.

- Let the head feel as if it is resting deep in the water relaxing the neck muscles. Halfway through the roll, the left ear should feel as if it is attached to the left shoulder.

- Press the right shoulder back and scull deeply with the right hand as the layover begins. Delay putting the right foot into the water, holding it briefly above the surface just before it touches.

(Cont.)

Common Errors (cont.)

- Right leg sets deeply in the water in an underextended position (short of the 90-degree pike).
- Left leg pikes forward or arches back during Layover.

Corrections (cont.)

- Pull the right leg up toward the left shoulder halfway through the Layover.
- Keep the hips tight and the pressure up to the surface on the left leg. The left leg and hips should feel like they are rolling on a "barbecue stick."

Elevator Action
Vertical to Double Submarine by Pike Up

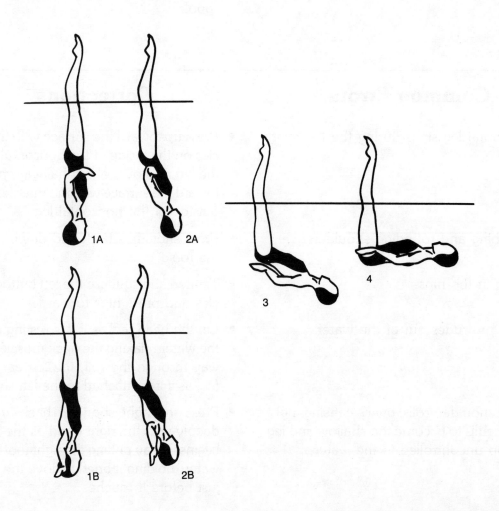

This action is part of the Elevator and High-tower figures. For convenience, it will be called the Elevator Action. The Elevator pike-up should be done slowly and smoothly, at the same tempo as the rest of the figure, with the back remaining quite straight. It is not a "roll-up" with a rounded back. The legs should remain perfectly stationary through the pike-up, with absolutely no change in water level, up or down, or movement forward or backward. There should be no traveling.

Two techniques are presented here. The first is preferred because it provides the swimmer with more control and a capability for maintaining very high water levels during the Elevator Action. However, it also seems to give the swimmers a sense of insecurity. A greater number of swimmers use the second technique even though they are far more likely to have problems using it.

Method of Execution: Technique Number One

To begin, the body should be Vertical with the head downward. A Support scull is used to maintain the water level. Height is desirable on the Elevator Action, and this technique works best if the swimmer tries to hold her legs slightly above her buoyancy level. However, the initial level should be one that the swimmer can hold comfortably throughout the pike-up.

With a slightly exaggerated outward scull, the shoulders and head are pulled slightly in front of the hips. The swimmer should not consciously use the abdominal muscles or the hip flexors to bend the hips. The hands should be turned over immediately on the return (inward) scull into a Standard scull action (palms facing the bottom) just below hip level. Wrists should be flexed to keep the fingers pointing downward and to prevent traveling. Turning the hands over and back to the hip area will press the shoulders forward still further. Deliberate movement using the abdominal muscles and/or hip flexors will not be necessary. The swimmer should get the feeling of sculling *only* to lift the hips and legs upward

as if she were disengaging the body from the legs. The chest and head should be allowed to *float* upward without any effort. Rather than letting the abdominal muscles tighten, the swimmer should try to get the feeling of pushing the small of the back forward through the stomach. The sculling action is continued, with the elbows well flexed, until the head and shoulders reach the same level as the hips. The abdomen, hips, and thighs should tighten to maintain and lock the torso and legs into the 90-degree Double Submarine position.

As stated above, this technique seems to give the swimmer some feeling of insecurity, even though it actually provides maximum control. She will need some encouragement to use it. Tell her how well it works, or she is likely to choose the overhead sculling action used in the second technique. A swimmer who is switching to this technique after using the overhead scull for the Elevator Action may initially frantically reverse her arms by alternately pressing and pulling.

Method of Execution: Technique Number Two

Beginning in a Vertical position with head facing downward, the swimmer uses an overhead Torpedo-like scull with her hands at about ear level to maintain stability. The water level should be at buoyancy level. If it is held much higher, most swimmers will execute an unstable Elevator Action (except for those few whose body structure provides unusual support in the hips). The Pike-Up is begun by pressing back with the hands slightly to move the head and shoulders forward a little in front of the hips. It is important that the hip flexors and abdominal muscles not be tightened to make the move. The swimmer should feel as if the small of the back is being moved forward through the stomach and then upward. The chest and head should float. The same overhead sculling action is continued, primarily to hold stability. The hands move back behind the head, still close to the shoulders, as the head rises. When the body reaches about the 45-degree angle, the swimmer should shift from an overhead scull to a Standard scull at the hips. The best time to make this shift will vary with the flotation distribution of the swimmer. Younger slim girls without much hip and buttock padding may have to make the shift earlier to prevent a change in the water level on the legs. Girls with low density structure may be able to continue the overhead scull at head level all the way to the 90-degree position. The rise of the head and shoulders must be relaxed until the head reaches the same level as the hips. The abdomen, hip and thigh muscles should tighten to maintain and lock the torso and legs into the 90-degree Double Submarine position.

Teaching Progression

In the Water Have the Swimmers:

1. Assume a Vertical position with the head downward and the back against the side of the pool. To keep the swimmers stable, have a partner hold the feet at their buoyancy level. The swimmers should press the head and shoulders slightly forward away from the wall. They may need to apply slight pressure with their elbows or hands, for Support or Torpedo scull respectively, to move the head and shoulders. Next, they should allow the chest to float the rest of the torso up to the 90-degree pike without sculling. A key phrase to repeat to your swimmers is: "Let the water do all of the work!"

2. Assume the same Vertical position as above against the side of the pool. Repeat the same procedure without a partner. The swimmers may only scull for stability.

If the legs fall away from the wall, it is because the body was brought up with the leg and stomach muscles instead of allowing the water to float the body up. The water level on the legs may drop in this drill, which is okay.

3. Assume the same Vertical position as in Number 1 above. After the swimmers execute Number 2 successfully, add one of the sculling actions described in the Method of Execution section.

4. Assume a Vertical position away from the wall. Using a partner to keep the legs in vertical alignment, have them repeat Number 3 above using the same sculling technique they practiced.

5. Execute the Elevator Action away from the wall without a partner.

Common Errors	**Corrections**
• Legs fall over the face.	• Almost always caused by trying to draw the body toward the legs by tightening abdominal and hip flexor muscles. Learn to relax and press the back and abdomen forward, rather than tightening and curling.
• Getting stuck part of the way up on the pike-up.	• Usually caused from trying to scull with the shoulders rather than with the elbows (in the first technique). Elbows must be well flexed to allow the scull to move from under the buttocks and out, much like the scull used in the Roll-Lift.
• Traveling.	• Hand angles are wrong in the sculling. With the Standard scull (Technique 1), finger tips must be pointing down. With the scull at ear level (Technique 2), palms must be facing *toward* the shoulders, not away.
• Changing levels.	• The weight above the water does not remain matched to the floating power or the supporting scull. In the first technique, the Standard scull must be at a steady rate, with a constant pressure supporting the legs. In the second technique, the swimmer must shift to the Standard scull soon enough to provide support for the hips and legs after the floating support of the chest can no longer go directly to the legs. Abrupt level changes usually result from sudden muscle contractions to try to lift the body and will generally be accompanied by the legs falling over the face.

Swordasub Action
Bent Knee Archover to Ballet Leg

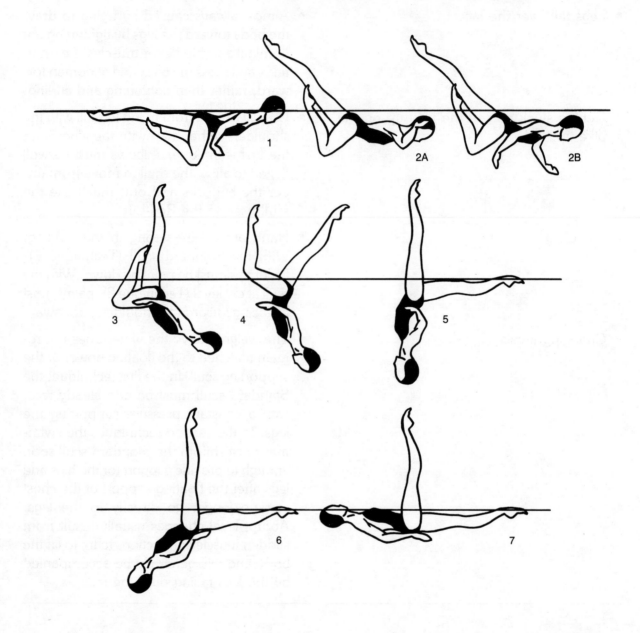

This action is very specific to the Swordasub skill. However, using it in a hybrid can add interest to the movement. The following two techniques describe the execution of the Bent Knee Archover to Ballet Leg.

The Swordasub Action starts just like a Swordfish, but midway through the Archover movement, the bent leg must begin to straighten vertically. The leg must be fully extended to the vertical by the time the foot of the straight leg has reached the surface at the end of the Archover. From that point, the head and shoulders are lifted to bring the body horizontal to a standard Ballet Leg position. Although the figure description in the 1985-86 rulebook does not actually specify this, it is generally accepted that the foot of the horizontal leg should remain at the surface during the lift of the body and not sink under the surface.

Two basic arm actions are generally used for beginning the Archover from the Bent Knee Layout position. The first is a symmetrical press-lift, using both arms simultaneously. The second is a paddle action in which each arm alternates the press. In both actions, the Archover is a rotation of the legs and torso around the hips, not a lift of the hips and legs. As a result, the initial arm presses are actually used to pull the chest under the water, not to lift the legs and hips.

Method of Execution: Technique Number One

The swimmer assumes a Front Layout position, takes a breath, and places her face in the water. She should stop sculling momentarily to float relaxed and in place. The arms are moved forward slowly and gently, to about a 45-degree angle toward the bottom of the pool. The hands are placed either directly under the shoulders or in front of them. The elbows should remain slightly bent. To get the feeling of starting to lift the toe of the extended leg out of the water without using any arm action, simply by arching, tighten the buttock muscles. Then tighten the back of the leg. The arms begin to press only after the swimmer has started this lift with the back of the leg. For this technique, the swimmer should try to get the feeling of grasping the water for support in arching the leg over. The hands should be pressed directly up toward

the surface, passing by the ears, and then moved to the outside of the shoulders. At the same time, the back and hips are arched strongly to make the foot of the extended leg rise from the water. With proper coordination of the back arch and arm press, the extended leg should be almost vertical by the time the hands pass by the head. The hands can then be moved quickly to a Support scull in front of the body with a small circular recovery. The Support scull is used to complete the lift, as well as for most of the remainder of the Archover. Beginners may require a second press which they start right in front of the face by pulling the arms back quickly with elbows bent. The press and recovery are done almost entirely with the elbows. The shoulders work only to make the upper arms follow the elbows.

Method of Execution: Technique Number Two

Technique 2 uses the same beginning as the first technique. The toe lift is initiated before the arms begin to press from their forward, relaxed, extended position. After the toe has cleared the water surface, the first arm presses with the elbow. The first hand is brought back up toward the shoulder and to the ear. As that hand reaches the ear, the other hand be-

gins its press. The second hand is slightly farther ahead of the shoulder but still pressing up past the top of the head, while the first arm recovers from the ear to in front of the lower chest or near the hips. The first arm then presses forward and over the head as the second arm recovers. With experience, and a good arch and timing, three Paddle presses (sculls) should be enough to bring the extended leg to a nearly vertical position. Both arms are recovered to a Support scull action in front of the chest to complete the lift. Less experienced swimmers may need to make several more paddles to gain a stable position for the Support scull.

With either technique, the swimmer should shift her attention to the vertical extension of the bent knee as soon as she switches her hands to Support scull. The current rules specify that the bent knee extension should start as the extended leg reaches vertical. Just as the extended leg becomes vertical, the swimmer should begin pressing the bent leg upward, using a Support scull to keep the extended leg moving continuously and smoothly. She should feel as if the shin is pressing upward with the front of the thigh.

As the bent knee leg straightens and the extended leg moves farther toward the surface, the Support scull action must move from in front of the body to the side to provide support for the added weight above the hips.

The extension must continue, using the Support scull, until a Knight position is reached. Then the arms must be turned over to a Standard scull action to provide support for the vertical leg, while allowing the chest to float upward. Pressure from the Standard scull will also press the shoulders toward the surface. The swimmer must make an effort to keep her head from popping up too quickly. She should concentrate on keeping the hips and leg lifted high. In addition, she must keep the foot of the horizontal leg from sinking under the surface during the movement of the body.

Teaching Progression

In the Water Have the Swimmers:

1. Assume a Bent Knee Front Layout with the head almost touching the foot pads of a pool access ladder. (This exercise will help the swimmers get the feeling of using their back and rotating around the hips for the Archover.) They should place their hands under a rung they can reach easily without pulling their head under. Have them tighten the back of the straight leg and buttock. Using the rung to pull down, the swimmer should press the head under while arching strongly, until the head passes through the arms with the leg lifting high. The action can be continued, carefully, until the back rests against the ladder.

2. Use a partner in shallow water in the absence of a ladder. The partner should submerge her arms a little more than elbow deep. The swimmer holds and presses against her partner's arms at that depth to initiate the lift.
   Note: The Swordfish lift should be practiced and mastered before attempting the leg extension. Properly done, the Swordasub is not an easy figure. It is difficult to cure bad habits the swimmer acquires when she tries to do the Swordasub before she has the skill to perform it correctly.

3. Work with partners in shallow water. To get the feeling of the vertical leg extension, the partner should hold the swimmer's arching leg to keep it from continuing over too fast while the bent knee is extended. The partner's touch may also act as a signal that it is time, or past time, to start the extension. In addition, the partner may provide some support for the hips, if needed.

4. Practice the skill without a partner.

Common Errors	**Corrections**

- Archover is completed before the extension is completed.

- This is the most common problem, almost to the extent that it becomes the normal manner of execution. It generally results from poor support in the Archover. The Archover is completed too quickly and can only be corrected by learning the proper support for a slow, smooth, finish. This problem is also caused by poor timing of the extension—that is, starting too late, sometimes even after the Archover is complete. To correct it, begin thinking of and initiating the extension as soon as the Support scull is started.

- The leg extends into a Split position instead of a Knight position.

- This is generally caused by using the stomach for the extension, and is often accompanied by a loss of arch as the body is pulled forward to help extend the leg. Concentrate on using the front of the thigh to press the shin upward. Maintain the arch during the extension.

- The leg sinks as the hips "sit" into the water.

- This is a problem of support that requires practice to learn how to provide a strong Support scull. Continue Support scull throughout the latter part of the action. Sitting also occurs when the swimmer changes too soon from the Support scull to the Standard scull. This makes the head and chest pop up while the hips settle down. Try to achieve a Knight position before shifting to the Standard scull.

Note: Many other problems occur prior to the start of the leg extension, but those are also common to the Straight Leg Swordfish and are covered in that section, pages 12-15.

Roll-Lift Action

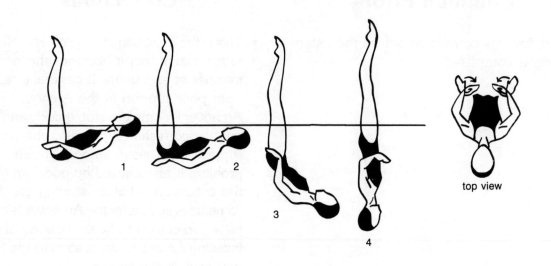

top view

A Roll-Lift (unroll) is simply rolling the body into a straight position. In synchronized swimming, this skill is used when the body moves from a piked (as in a Barracuda) to a Vertical position. The technique presented here can be used in all figures that include this kind of movement.

Method of Execution

To begin the Roll-Lift, the swimmer squeezes her hips forward, tucking them under the body, and stretches the buttocks upward (as if a hand is pressing from underneath up on the tailbone). Tightening the hips together will force the face underwater. She relaxes the upper stomach and stretches her chest to allow her torso to "fall away" from the extended leg(s). The swimmer then begins contracting the lower abdomen into the spine. Once the Roll-Lift is initiated, the buttocks must be constantly squeezed together and forward. The swimmer should not round the shoulders or tuck the chin. She presses down with the back of the head and neck to help press the torso down, watching that the head and shoulders do not arch. The toes of the vertical leg(s) reach upward. The hands begin sculling in a stationary Standard scull and almost immediately change to a deeper Reverse scull as the Roll-Lift begins. During the Roll-Lift the palms should remain parallel to the bottom of the pool, which will require more wrist flexion as the torso moves deeper. As the back unrolls, vertebra by vertebra, beginning with the lower back, the torso should fall through the hands so that they do not move back behind the torso. The swimmer then tightens the thigh of the extended leg(s) and pushes the knee cap(s) through the back of the leg(s). Pointing the toes of the vertical leg(s) too hard will sometimes cause the knees to bend. The back of the leg should be stretched from the hip to the ankle. At about the two-thirds point of the Roll-Lift, on an outward scull, the hands make a circle out to the sides (like a small Breaststroke pull). The swimmer must be careful not to reach behind the torso. She circles her hands around and, on the inward scull, flips them over into a Support scull. The flip-over should be made by circling the fingers inward and then out to the side, with the fingers always leading the wrist as the hands turn over fully. As this circle scull is made, it may be necessary to flex the wrists and feel like the entire body is being pulled forward to prevent backward movement into the "catch." This circle promotes the desired rise or lift into the Vertical position. At the time of the catch, the swimmer must continue to tighten the stomach hard against the spine, squeeze the buttocks, and pull the ribcage in and down. The front side of the torso is shortened to avoid a hyperextended chest and to prevent the shoulders from unrolling past vertical. A full body and leg stretch is necessary at this point for better extension, height, and control.

Teaching Progression

On the Deck Have the Swimmers:

1. Sit with their legs together and extended. To begin the Roll-Lift, they should imagine a brick has been placed lengthwise on their chests between the breasts and is pressing the chest down. Next, they should collapse their abdomens into the small of their backs and unroll the torso one vertebra at a time to reach a Back Layout position.

2. Stand and pike at the hips until their trunks are parallel to the deck. The swimmers should then perform the correct arm action and unroll the back at the appropriate time.

In the Water Have the Swimmers:

1. Hold onto the gutter and extend their legs up and over the side of the pool. They should pretend that an imaginary iron bar has been placed in front of the shins and in back of the calves to hold the legs in place. Their backs should face the bottom of the pool. From this position, have them practice the unrolling action so that the back straightens down the side of the pool, one vertebra at a time. They should keep in mind the feeling of the brick on the chest. The swimmers should stop when the torso is in a Vertical (head downward) in line with the thighs and the side of the pool.

2. Practice the Roll-Lift while a partner holds the legs in a Vertical position in chest-deep water away from the wall. Remind them to think about the brick and to unroll one vertebra at a time.

3. Practice the Roll-Lift without support, using correct body and sculling techniques described.

Common Errors

- Legs rock over the face during the Roll-Lift.

Corrections

- Loosen the hip joint at the beginning. Round the back and unroll one vertebra at a time. Tighten the buttocks and back of the thighs of the extended legs. Press the hips forward during the Roll-Lift. Let the face and chest fall away from the surface at the beginning. Imagine an iron bar is placed in front of the shins, holding the legs in place.

(Cont.)

Common Errors (cont.)	Corrections (cont.)
• Attempting to move into the Vertical position by pushing the shoulders back instead of unrolling.	• Collapse the abdomen into the small of the back and unroll one vertebra at a time.
• Attempting to move into the Vertical by pushing the hips back over the head instead of unrolling the torso under the hips.	• Unroll the torso instead of pushing the shoulders back and flex the wrists during the Roll-Lift.
• Becoming stuck about halfway through the Roll-Lift and having difficulty completing or going on.	• Use more pelvic tilt (stomach and buttock contractions). Keep the head and shoulders in the same alignment, bend the elbows, and scull with just the lower arm and hands (use more wrist action).
• Traveling head-first during the Roll-Lift.	• Flex the wrist more and more as the body submerges. Feel like the scull is foot first.
• No rise or lift during the Roll-Lift.	• The circle that is made toward the end of the Roll-Lift should be stronger in order to lift the hips. Make sure this circle presses out and toward the bottom of the pool.
• Hyperextension of the chest, causing the shoulders to unroll too far at the end or the vertical leg to press the body onto the back.	• The circle scull and catch should be made sooner. Catch to the side, not in front of the torso. Tighten the stomach muscles and press the belly button into the small of the back during the catch to Support scull. Tighten the front side of the body during the catch. Keep the front of the thigh tight. Feel like the body is short of the Vertical position.

Bent Knee Join to Vertical

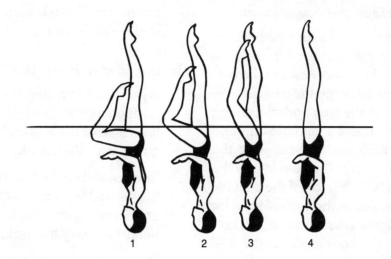

The Bent Knee Join to Vertical is another very important skill for the aspiring synchronized swimmer to master. Some figures include this action while twisting before the figure is completed as in the Nova and the Albatross. The swimmer must learn and per-fect this skill stationary before attempting it while twisting. Other figures, such as the Bent Knee Flamingo, include this action in a stationary position. The following techniques should be used to learn this action.

Method of Execution

The action begins in Support scull in a Bent Knee Vertical. The scull in the Bent Knee Vertical will be slightly in front of the body to support the bent knee weight on the front side of the body. On an inward scull, the swimmer begins the extension of the bent knee by sliding the bent-knee foot up with the achilles and the thigh up with the front of the thigh muscle. The toe should stay toward the front of the leg while sliding to prevent it from going behind the vertical leg. As the bent knee rises, the tempo and pressure of the scull will increase and the elbows will pull slightly toward the back so that center balance support is maintained with the hands nearer the hips. The elbows stay close to the hips. If the swimmer has very good external rotation of the forearm, she can achieve center balance support by keeping her elbows in and moving her hands back. In either case, the movement of the arms from the shoulders should be isolated. The stomach is pulled into the spine and the rib cage rolled down. During the extension, the swimmer should concentrate on holding the vertical leg stationary by keeping the thigh and buttocks tight. Just prior to the finish of the leg Join, the foot pauses. The Join is finished by a tilt of the hips and a stretch of the thigh and buttock of the bent knee, along with increased pressure and tempo of the scull. At this point, a super leg and torso stretch is needed for extra stability and control. The swimmer should imagine a high water level to give the impression of extra height and strength.

Teaching Progression

On the Deck Have the Swimmers:

1. Stand against the wall with one leg bent so that the big toe touches the opposite leg just above the knee. Assume the correct posture by flattening the back against the wall, tucking the hips under, keeping the shoulders relaxed and down, and pressing the neck and head against the wall. Slide the foot of the bent leg up the vertical leg with the big toe of the bent leg touching the inside of the vertical leg. Use a pelvic tilt, tighten the stomach and buttocks to keep the back as flat to the wall as possible. The swimmers should practice this several times on each leg.

2. Practice moving the hands back and forth in a Support scull, increasing the tempo as the legs come close to touching. The swimmers should keep an even-paced scull in-and-out movement.

In the Water Have the Swimmers:

1. Assume an inverted Bent Knee Vertical position against the wall by flattening the back against the wall and holding onto the gutter with the hands.

2. Practice sliding the foot of the bent leg up the vertical leg, emphasizing the pelvic tilt and keeping the back, shoulders, and head touching the wall.

3. Practice the Join several times away from the wall with a partner holding the vertical leg in place.

4. Practice the Join away from the wall without a partner.

Common Errors	Corrections
• Sitting or piking during the Join.	• Stretch the thigh of the vertical leg on the front side. Press the hips forward, keeping the buttocks very tight, and use a pelvic tilt to Join.
• Arching vertical leg or back.	• Concentrate on the vertical leg to keep it stationary. Pull the stomach into the small of the back and shorten the front side of the torso.
• Traveling backwards during the Join.	• Flex the wrists and elbows and feel as though you are pulling your hips forward to make the Join.
• Chest hyperextends and shoulders arch out toward the end of the Join.	• Keep the stomach pulled into the spine and the rib cage rolled down. Relax the back of the shoulders halfway through the Join. Isolate the leg movement from the torso by stabilizing the body position in the Bent Knee Vertical position. Make sure the top leg is not closing forward to meet the joining leg toward the end of the Join.

Crane Join to Vertical

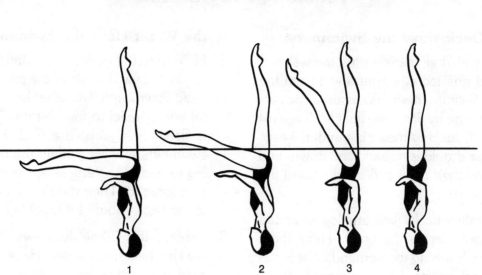

1   2   3   4

The Crane Join action is used in many of the required figures as well as in hybrids. The swimmer should use the following technique any time she is in a Crane position and must close her legs to a Vertical. This action becomes more important after the swimmer has attained a higher level of skill.

Method of Execution

The swimmer begins in a Crane position (see *Coaching Synchronized Swimming Effectively,* pp. 94-95) and will move to a vertical position by joining the horizontal leg up to the vertical leg.

The hands begin a Support scull with the arms slightly in front of the hips to help support and balance the horizontal leg. Before lifting the leg, the stomach, shoulders, and head should be set into their correct vertical positions and alignment and frozen. The belly button is pressed into the back bone. Tightening and squeezing the back of the horizontal leg and buttocks, the swimmer presses up with her knee cap so it feels like the knee is lifting before the foot. On an outward scull, she stretches or reaches with the horizontal leg. On the next inward scull, the leg lift is begun by further tightening the buttock and

thigh of the horizontal leg. To lift the knee from the surface, the swimmer reaches very slightly underneath her knee with the Support scull, then moves her hands back beside the hips for proper balance as the leg rises closer to the Vertical. The speed of the scull will increase, and the size of the sculls should decrease. These sculls should be kept even and smooth. Keeping the belly button pressed into the small of the back will hold the shoulders in line. Toward the end of the close, the swimmer should slow the movement of the leg slightly and press the hips forward as the stomach tightens and presses into the back to squeeze the leg in line. A super stretch of the legs and torso will make the swimmer look taller and give the impression of extra height and strength. She should concentrate on keeping the vertical leg very still and steady during the Join.

Teaching Progression

On the Deck Have the Swimmers:

1. Stand with their backs against the wall and extend one leg at a right angle from the body. Swimmers should assume the correct posture by flattening their back against the wall, tucking their hips under, keeping their shoulders relaxed and down, and pressing their neck and head against the wall.

2. Lie on their backs with one leg extended perpendicular to the body. Have them practice lowering the perpendicular leg as a partner resists the movement.

3. Practice the correct sculling technique with the proper timing on the Crane Join movement described above.

In the Water Have the Swimmers:

1. Hold onto the gutter and extend one leg vertically over the side of the pool with the head downward. The other leg is horizontal and parallel to the bottom. The back is flattened against the wall. Have the swimmers practice joining the horizontal leg to meet the vertical leg, pressing the hips forward. Their shoulders, head, and lower back should be touching the wall.

2. Practice the Crane Join away from the wall in chest-deep water. Have a partner hold the vertical leg in place.

3. Practice the Crane Join away from the wall in deep water without supports.

Common Errors

- Sitting or piking during the Crane Join.

- Arching the torso or vertical leg during the movement.

- Traveling backwards during the Crane Join.

Corrections

- Stretch the horizontal leg out in front and press the hips forward to Join. Tighten the buttock of the vertical leg.

- Concentrate on the vertical leg to keep it stationary. Pull the stomach into the small of the back and tighten the front side of the torso. Do not allow the scull to reach too far forward.

- Flex the wrists and bend the elbows on the Support scull. The hips should feel as if they are being pulled forward to make the Join. The hands should be flat to the bottom of the pool on the in scull and rotated way to the back on the out scull. Accentuate the out scull over the in scull.

(Cont.)

Common Errors (cont.)

- Chest hyperextends and shoulders arch toward the end of the Join.

Corrections (cont.)

- Keep the stomach pulled in and the ribcage pulled down during the leg lift. Relax the back of the shoulders. Keep the head in line. Isolate the leg movement from the torso. Set and freeze the body in the Crane position. Make sure the vertical leg is not coming forward to meet the joining leg toward the end of the Join.

Chapter 3: Ending Actions

Ending actions in synchronized swimming are those skills used to complete the figure. Because they are the last part of a figure that a judge, coach, or spectator sees, ending actions leave the final impression of a swimmer's performance. Although there are numerous ways to complete a figure or hybrid, this chapter presents the three that are the most important for coaches to work on with intermediate-level swimmers. The Walkout to Back Layout is a fairly common and frequently used skill by swimmers starting at the grass-roots level. Once mastered, the Walkout can help make the difference between an average and a good score in competition. The Archover to a Back Layout offers some new challenges to the swimmer and coach. When her performance becomes consistent, the swimmer can use this aesthetically pleasing action as a method for finishing some hybrids. The Vertical Descent is a critical skill to master. Without it, a swimmer cannot spin or twist.

Walkout to Back Layout

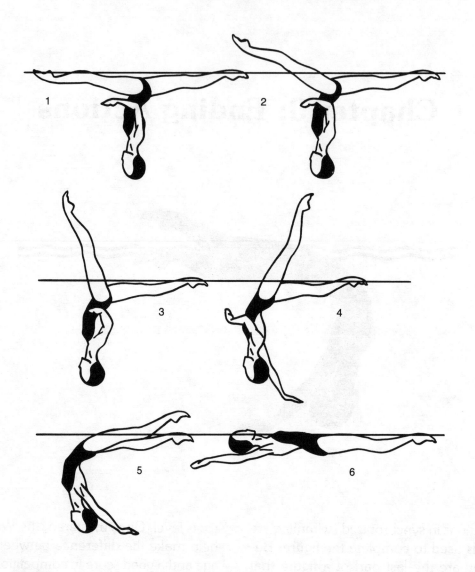

Coaching Synchronized Swimming Effectively describes a beginning to intermediate-level method for the Walkout. The following, more advanced procedure for a Walkout uses a "split-arm" technique. This technique provides for better balance, height, and control.

For it to be used, however, the swimmer must be at an advanced enough level of body awareness, strength, and control to keep the hips in proper alignment as the hands move to a split-arm position.

Method of Execution

In as many cases as possible, the right leg should be used as the Walkout leg. It is stronger than the left leg on most swimmers, and having the right leg forward in the Split

position usually produces a wider Split.

From the Split position, the front leg is stretched out in front as the hips press forward. The hands are in a Support scull, reaching slightly forward under the closing leg to initiate the close and provide support. The thigh of the back leg must press toward the bottom as the shin presses upward and the toe point relaxes slightly to prevent the back knee from bending. The back leg should feel as if it is being pulled into the hip or shortened to create a pivot point. The moving leg should feel as if it is stretching forward and describing an arc with a radius slightly larger than the length of the leg. This will force the swimmer to really stretch her leg so that her toe will touch the arc. The front leg should be pressed up with the front of the thigh so that it feels like the leg, thigh, and the knee are lifting first, followed by the foot. The arms are in a Support scull with the elbows pulled in close to the hips. The swimmer should feel as if her arms are pulling her body face first at the beginning to prevent backward travel. As the leg lifts, the hands move more to the sides and in back of the hips with the elbows back and bent. The main arch should be in the hips and lower back, not in the upper back or shoulders. As the leg moves past the vertical, the swimmer should use the muscles in the back of the leg, pressing up and tightening the thigh to lower the leg slowly. After the leg passes the Knight position (at about 2 o'clock) the left arm (on most swimmers—some use the right arm) presses back and

toward the bottom of the pool to provide lift of the hips. The arm then moves overhead and in back of the shoulders to a strong Torpedo scull with the hand flexed and elbow bent. The other hand moves out in front of the chest, perpendicular to the surface. The palm is facing the feet in an effort to pull the body and hips forward, away from the wall toward which the leg is moving. As the leg comes closer to the surface, the stomach tightens, the buttocks squeeze forward, and the back begins to roll up, releasing the arch. If the arch in the back is too deep, it will pull the hips down. The swimmer should feel as if she is setting her knee into the surface before her foot and then delay her foot briefly above the surface before allowing it to enter the water. The right hand then evens out to join the left and transfers overhead into a Torpedo scull. Depending on the momentum of the foot-first movement, the hands should change to a Dolphin scull to slow the surfacing action of the chest, shoulders, and face. There should be just enough movement foot-first to continue the natural flow of the figure, making sure the head ends up where the hips began in the split position. The body rolls to the surface, leading with the hips, followed by the stomach, the chest, the shoulders, and finally the face. During this sequence, the hips squeeze, and the legs shorten.

Teaching Progression

In the Water Have the Swimmers:

1. Assume a Split position facing away from the side of the pool and supporting the back leg on the pool gutter. Have them lift the front leg in an arc to join the leg resting on the gutter.

2. Assume a Split position facing the side of the pool and supporting the front leg on the pool gutter. Have them lift the leg

resting on the gutter in an arch to join the other leg and perform the Dolphin scull to assume the Back Layout position.

3. Assume an arched position with the hips at the surface, split the arms, and try to scull the hips forward. They should Dolphin scull with the palms of the hands facing the body and the forearms parallel to the surface. Have them swing from the

elbows using a great deal of in-and-out lateral wrist movement. They should do lengths of this headfirst scull to strengthen the scull.

4. Assuming the same arched position, place one hand (most use the left) in back of the shoulders between the shoulder blades, and Dolphin scull with the other hand, palm facing the body and the forearm parallel to the surface. Have them do lengths of this down the pool following the lane lines to keep their movement straight.

5. Place their feet on the gutter at the side of the pool. Assume the same arched position, hips remaining at the surface and place one hand on the stomach (most use the right). Then they should Torpedo scull with the left hand (palm facing flat to the bottom) in an effort to stay in one place.

6. Move off the wall in the same arched position, with the left hand in Torpedo scull, palm facing the bottom of the pool, and the right arm stretched out in front of the body, forearm parallel to the surface and palm facing the chest. Using both arms, they should try to move down the pool head first. Tell them to concentrate on keeping the shoulders and hips in alignment so there is no twisting, tipping, or side arching. Have the swimmers do lengths of this.

7. Practice the Walkout with the back of the upper thigh of the back leg resting on a lane line using the split-arm technique.

8. Practice the Walkout away from the lane line.

Note: The split-arm technique is for intermediate to advanced swimmers. The beginner must first learn to use a great deal of hip arch, with arms extending overhead in back of the shoulders in a Torpedo scull with bent elbows and flexed hands. As flexibility and body control increase, the swimmer can add the Dolphin scull after the feet close in order to slow down foot-first travel to the Back Layout position.

Common Errors

- Not enough stretch or hip and lower back arch.

- Hips sink as leg is lifting.

- Splashing when lifting the leg.

- Excessive foot-first movement at the beginning.

- Extreme foot-first movement at the end of the figure.

- Too much arch in the upper back at end of the Walkout, pulling hips deep.

Corrections

- Before the leg lift occurs, make sure the splits are fully stretched and the arch is in the lower back.

- Strong pressure scull is needed for the first half of the lift.

- Make sure the leg is on the surface at the beginning.

- Bend the elbows and wrists so that you feel as if you are pulling your face forward during the first half of the lift.

- Control movement with the split-arm technique and Dolphin scull with the hands behind the head.

- Release the arch in the back toward the end and float the back up.

(Cont.)

Common Errors (cont.)

- Tightening in the torso as the hands move into the split-arm technique.

- Splashing when lowering the leg.

- Feet sinking after they meet.

Corrections (cont.)

- Twist the torso the opposite way to counteract. Use body control to hold the hips, torso, and shoulders in correct alignment.

- Tighten the front of the thigh as the leg comes closer to the surface. Delay touching the foot to the surface at the end.

- Press the toes up to the surface with the underneath leg muscles. Do not try to pull the head up to the surface too quickly.

Bent Knee Archover to Back Layout (Knight)

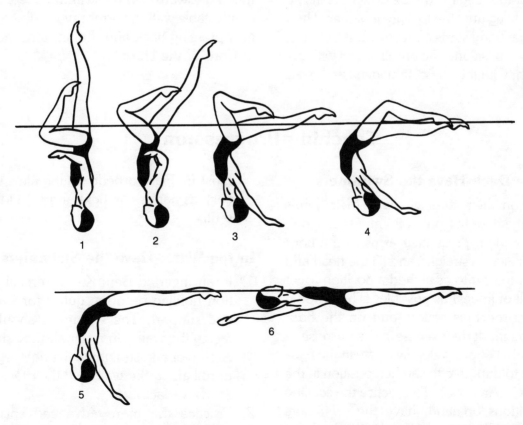

The Bent Knee Archover to the Back Layout action is used in both the Knight and the Swordfish. In addition it can be used in routines in which a hybrid is executed in shallow water. The technique taught here is for those swimmers who have gained control over their bodies in the water. Another technique is also described for the more advanced athlete.

Method of Execution

Before the Archover at the end of the Knight figure, the body is in a Bent Knee Vertical position with the left leg straight and the right knee bent. This is because the figure begins in a right Ballet Leg. The arms are Support sculling with the elbows close to the torso. The head, hip, and ankle of the vertical leg are in line with the body. As the body begins to arch, beginning in the upper back and proceeding to the lower back, the elbows reach back behind the hips. As the left leg begins to press down toward the surface in an extremely arched position, both arms move from a Support scull position to a Torpedo scull. The palms should face the bottom of the pool, with the head also looking down at the bottom and positioned as far under the back of the knees as possible. In this position, the right foot begins to slide down the inside of the left leg until the legs are together. Then the upper body starts a reverse Roll-Lift from an arched position. The unroll begins with the stomach, with the chest, shoulders, and head

following to the surface. Dolphin scull is used to stop excessive forward movement and to enable the back to simply float up into a Back Layout position.

Advanced swimmers can learn to use a split-arm technique to keep the hips stable and cut down on foot-first movement. As the body arches and the left leg passes the 2 o'clock position, the left arm presses back and toward the bottom of the pool to provide lift to the hips. The arm then moves up to a strong Torpedo scull with the hand flexed and elbow bent. The right hand moves out in front of the chest with the elbow slightly bent and the hand perpendicular to the surface. The palm faces the feet in an effort to pull the body and hips away from the wall that the leg is moving toward. Some swimmers feel more comfortable with the arms reversed, the right arm pressing back and the left arm moving in front of the chest.

Teaching Progression

On the Deck Have the Swimmers:

1. Lie on their stomachs with their hands on the floor in front of them. On a signal, have them press their arms to the floor with elbows straight, and lift the head and shoulders into as arched a position (over back of knees) as possible. (They should keep the hips square and on the floor throughout the exercise.) The purpose of this drill is to develop flexibility in the back and to duplicate the arched position in the Knight Archover. To practice the sculling positions on land, have the swimmers work with partners, who should check the arm positions in this order: (a) Support scull (elbows close to torso) (b) Support scull (elbows reaching back behind the

hips) (c) Flat Torpedo scull (palms as far back as hands can flex) and (d) Dolphin scull.

In the Water Have the Swimmers:

1. In an Inverted Bent Knee Vertical position holding onto the gutter for stability and support. The swimmers should be facing the wall. On a signal, they should Archover and straighten the right leg and unroll along the wall until their faces are at the surface.
2. Practice the more advanced split-arm technique by assuming an arched position with the hips at the surface, split the arms, and try to scull hips first. Have them do lengths of this sculling drill.

Common Errors

- Keeping elbows in as the body arches, causing traveling.
- Not pushing head back under the knees (in arched position).
- Palms not facing the bottom of the pool causing traveling.
- Letting the back come up at the same time as the leg, instead of unrolling from the Knight position.
- Torpedo sculling out to the Back Layout, resulting in excessive foot-first traveling.
- Feet sinking in the Back Layout after the unroll.

Corrections

- Reach as far back as possible with the elbows prior to the arch.
- Press the head as far under the back of the knees as possible to assume a good arched position.
- Palms must face the bottom of the pool in a flat sculling position.
- Make sure to straighten the right leg and then let the body unroll to the surface.
- Dolphin scull soon as the unroll to the surface begins.
- Keep the head back; tucking the chin forward too soon will make the feet sink.

Vertical Descent

The Vertical Descent is one of the most common actions seen in synchronized swimming. Beginning- and intermediate-level swimmers spend more time learning to exe-cute a good Vertical Descent than on most other skills. Swimmers should practice both of the following techniques for the Vertical Descent until they master one of them.

Method of Execution

This skill is executed from an Inverted Vertical position with a Support scull hold. Beginning at maximum height, the swimmer eases up slightly on the Support scull so that she starts to descend. As the descent continues, the scull must become easier and more to the side to maintain a continuous rate of descent. As the swimmer is easing up on the scull, the in scull does not come as far into the center line of the torso. The swimmer should isolate the upper arm movement so that she feels as if her torso is decending past the arms. The torso continues to move through the arms until the hands reach a totem pole position (an Inverted Torpedo scull). The swimmer should keep the elbows slightly in front of the shoulders and forearms, with the wrists flexed and in line with the head. Upon reaching her level of buoyancy, the swimmer's arm action must change to pull the toes beneath the surface. There are two good ways to achieve this;

have the swimmer try each to see which works best for her. In the first method, the swimmer simply turns her hands over so the palms face the surface of the water instead of the bottom of the pool just before she reaches the level of buoyancy. She continues sculling with her arms in this position until the toes have submerged. The second method also begins just prior to reaching the level of buoyancy. The swimmer gently slides her hands to a position overhead and then uses a Dolphin scull or small paddles to pull her toes beneath the surface of the water.

The buoyancy of the swimmer will dictate which method to use. More buoyant swimmers will find that the second method works best. For both methods it is important that the swimmer uses the least amount of hand movement to descend.

Teaching Progression

On the Deck Have the Swimmers:

1. Practice the first method of descent. Have them stand in correct posture with their arms performing Support scull motions. They should slow the scull down and gradually move the hands more to the sides, finally turning the palms over (toward the ground) and sculling in this position.

2. Practice the second method from Support scull, gradually slowing the sculls and moving the hands more to the sides. Extend the sculls up to shoulder level, slice the hands overhead, and practice Dolphin sculls or small paddles.

In the Water Have the Swimmers:

1. Review the Inverted Vertical position with

a Support scull.

2. If necessary, review the Inverted Vertical position and Support scull separately.

3. Assume an Inverted Vertical position against the pool wall with hands holding the gutter. They should let go and practice descending, keeping the head, back, hips, and legs against the wall.

4. Assume an Inverted Vertical position with Support scull in deep water. The swimmers should practice both methods of descent until they are fairly proficient in each and then choose the one that is most effective.

Note: It may be necessary for swimmers to change methods as their skills develop, so review both methods periodically.

Common Errors	**Corrections**
• Descent stops, slows down, speeds up rather than maintaining continuous speed.	• Increase or decrease pressure on the scull to adjust the speed.
• Stopping at buoyancy level.	• Change to one of the pulling under arm actions sooner.
• Body piking forward, feet on back as the buoyancy level is reached.	• Maintain body alignment by tightening muscles and stretching. Keep hands directly overhead for the first method or directly at sides of the body for the second. Increase scull to pull under slightly. It should feel like the body is sinking but the legs are stretching up.

Chapter 4: Rotations

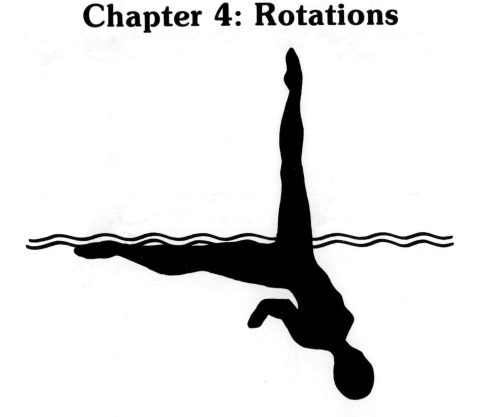

The two rotations presented in this chapter—the Catalina Rotation and the Reverse Catalina Rotation—are excellent skills for coaches to work on with intermediate swimmers. As the names of the skills suggest, one is the reverse of the other. However, the swimmer uses different techniques to execute each skill.

The Catalina Rotation is used in the Catalina Figures, the Subilarcs, and the Subalinas, all of which are good basic intermediate skills for figure competitions and routine construction. The Reverse Catalina is found in figure competitions and is also part of more difficult figures, such as the Dolpholina and the Castle.

Catalina Rotation

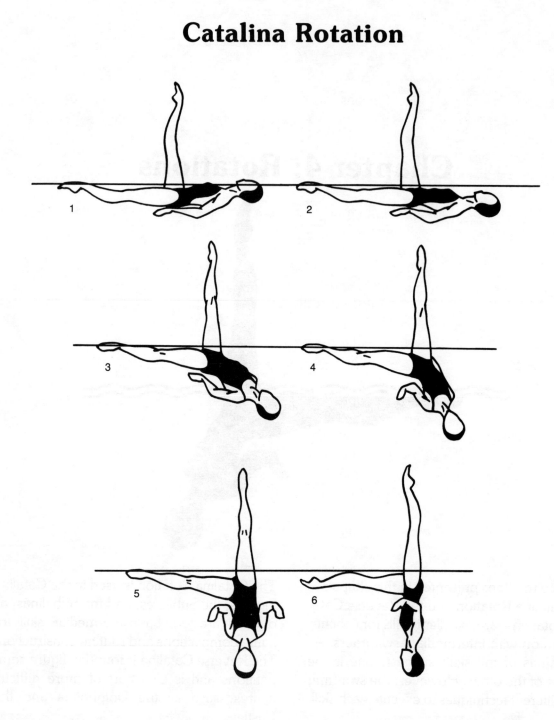

As previously mentioned, this skill is seen in the Catalina figures and is an excellent optional figure for the developing synchronized swimmer. Once the technique has been mastered, it can be applied to the other figures that include this Rotation; for example, the Subalinas and Subilarcs.

Method of Execution

The Catalina Rotation described here is for an extended right Ballet Leg and begins with a high Ballet Leg. Maintaining this height, the swimmer should allow the torso to drop slightly toward the bottom of the pool, applying pressure on the back of the head, neck, and shoulders. As her face is clearing the surface, she rolls her right leg in toward the center and her left leg out away from the center to begin the hip rotation. The swimmer should continue to lift the right leg higher and higher to prevent loss of height. The scull is deep and close to the hips. The left shoulder is dropped to the bottom and back under the right shoulder. The left ear should feel as if it is connected to the left shoulder. The torso will be taking a direct route—a spiraling action toward the bottom of the pool, passing through a side Crane position, with the torso directly beneath the hips. The torso continues to rotate so that it eventually reaches a Crane position. In a side Crane position, the legs and torso are turned 90 degrees to the side, with the torso directly beneath the hips and the legs as close to a 90-degree angle as possible.

During the Catalina Rotation, the wrist may need to flex to pull the body under the hips rather than the hips moving over the head. The hands are kept beside the hips and the right elbow is sharply bent. After the swimmer completes a third of the Rotation to the side Crane, on an outward scull, she should turn her left hand over to a Support scull. On the next out scull, the right hand is turned over to a Support scull. Slight pressure on the right leg out toward the baby toe will help the swimmer maintain balance until her body is directly beneath her hips. The swimmer should keep rotating the legs (right leg in, left leg out) to continue the hip rotation. Pressing the hips forward into the side Crane position will help prevent piking. The swimmer finishes the rotation in Support scull by rotating her legs and torso. From the beginning, she should feel as if her left hip is going to sink down under the right hip and come out on the other side in order to prevent side travel and right hip extension.

Teaching Progression

On the Deck Have the Swimmers:

1. Stand with the right leg extended at a right angle to the body, the heel resting on a support at the correct height. Practice rotating the right leg in and the torso to the left and toward the deck so that the torso is parallel to the deck.

2. Work with a partner during the Catalina Rotation to see that the swimmer's body is taking the most direct route to a horizontal position (no lateral movement).

3. Practice pressing the hips forward during the Rotation and achieving the correct

sequential timing of the arms as described in the Method of Execution.

4. Practice the Catalina Rotation using the correct sculling technique.

In the Water Have the Swimmers:

1. Stand on the left leg in shallow water with the foot of the right leg supported by the pool gutter or by a partner. Practice the Catalina Rotation using the same rotating motion as on the deck.

2. Place the right side of the body parallel to the wall and extend the right leg to the

Ballet Leg position. A partner standing on deck should hold the swimmer's right leg and right hand. Have the swimmer practice turning down to the side Crane position, trying to keep the back and shoulders against the wall while the partner holds her leg and hand. Repeat this several times. While maintaining contact with the vertical leg, have the partner let go of the swimmer's right hand as the swimmer rotates into the Crane position from the side Crane. Have them practice this as two distinct and separate movements.

3. Practice the Catalina Rotation from an extended Ballet Leg. Have one partner hold and rotate the vertical leg and another partner rotate and support the horizontal leg using the correct sculling action. Tell the swimmer to imagine a brick being placed on the chest to help sink the torso.

4. Practice the Catalina Rotation from an extended Ballet Leg with the foot of the horizontal leg resting on the gutter.

5. Practice the Catalina Rotation using the correct techniques.

Common Errors

- Leg comes over the face at the beginning of the rotation.

- Hands placing too much pressure on the surface at the beginning, causing the hips to rise.

- Arching and dropping back too far as a Knight take-down.

- Piking the hips and allowing the body to move laterally.

- Allowing the legs to move out of their respective planes (laterally).

Corrections

- While maintaining a high Ballet Leg position, allow the torso to drop slightly toward the bottom of the pool. Relax the hip and right leg angle. Put pressure on the extended leg away from the face.

- Use a deeper scull to initiate the Catalina Rotation. Use the hands only for support. Initiate the Catalina Rotation with the legs rather than the hands.

- Begin rotating and turning the legs in their sockets (right leg in, left leg out) as soon as the face clears the surface. Drop the left shoulder to the bottom sooner and back under the right shoulder.

- Maintain a high Ballet Leg from the start. Press the hips forward and feel that they are arching slightly. Lift the right leg over the left hip. Press the left shoulder back under the right.

- Feel as though the knees are turning the legs. Press the hips forward; piking during the rotation will cause the legs to drift out of line. Have partners hold the vertical and horizontal legs in place during the rotation. Tighten in the hips and squeeze the legs into the pelvic area. (Shorten the legs, especially the left leg, into the pelvic area.)

(Cont.)

Common Errors (cont.)

- Sculling the hips over the head instead of the body dropping under the hips.

- Thrusting the hips out at the beginning.

Corrections (cont.)

- Flex the wrists and elbows at the beginning.

- Slowly tighten the hips to control the speed of the figure.

Reverse Catalina Rotation

The Reverse Catalina is a figure by itself that is started from a Front Layout position. Once the swimmer is showing consistent perfor-mance of this skill, the coach can encourage her to attempt the more difficult figures that also include this action.

Method of Execution

This Reverse Catalina transition is begun in a Crane position with a Support scull. The right leg is vertical and the left leg is extended horizontally and perpendicular to the body. The Reverse Catalina Rotation is begun by pressing back slightly toward the heel on the vertical leg and toward the bottom of the pool on the horizontal leg. At the same time, the right leg is rolled outward and the left leg inward to start turning the hips. The body is rotated using a Support scull. The right elbow is behind the body with the hand out to the side. The swimmer keeps pressing the legs away from each other during the Rotation and opens the hips. Pressing back on the right shoulder, she pulls upward on the left. The hips are pressed forward (pelvic tilt) to eliminate any piking as the body passes through the side Crane position. The horizontal leg must press toward the bottom of the pool and the vertical leg out to the outside of the leg to maintain the proper balance and the 90-degree angle of the legs when passing through the side Crane position. In a side Crane position, the legs and torso are rotated 90 degrees to the side, with the torso directly beneath the hips and the legs in as close to a 90-degree angle as possible. After passing through the side Crane position, on an inward scull, the swimmer should turn the right hand over to a Standard scull. On the next inward scull, she should immediately turn the left hand over to a Standard scull. The hands should turn over before the body rolls onto the back. The swimmer then begins moving the right shoulder toward the surface and bends in at the waist on the right side. The right elbow must stay behind the right hip, the left hand ahead of the left hip, and the hands even with the hips (not over the head or near the shoulders). Even though the left hip is still slightly deeper than the right at this point, the hands must be at equal levels from the surface for proper support and to avoid sideways travel. While the hands turn over, the hips are held in place and then very gently rotated along with the shoulders. During this transfer of hands, the swimmer should keep arching the hips forward and extending the right leg as high out of the water as possible to avoid loss of height. Once the body is on the back, the momentum toward the surface can be paused by pressing back on the back of the neck, head, and shoulders and up on the hips. The swimmer releases the pressure of the horizontal leg toward the bottom of the pool to enable her face and the foot of the horizontal leg to surface at the same time. This will help prevent the head from "popping out" at the end. The swimmer then sculls up to a Ballet Leg position using an even-paced scull.

Teaching Progression

On the Deck Have the Swimmers:

1. Turn their backs to a chair and bend over at a right angle, extending the right leg back parallel to the deck. The top of the right foot should rest on the seat of the chair. Have them practice the Reverse Catalina Rotation, rotating the right leg out and turning the torso up to a vertical position facing the chair. The right leg should still be extended, with the heel resting on the seat of the chair.

2. Repeat the exercise above using a partner to check that the torso is taking the most direct route (no lateral movement) up to a standing position.

3. Practice using the arms in the correct sequential timing with the body rotation and

pressing the hips forward during the Rotation as described above.

In the Water Have the Swimmers:

1. Practice the Reverse Catalina Rotation standing in hip-level water with the back of the left leg facing the wall. The right leg should be extended back to rest the top of the foot on the gutter. The body should by lying face-down on the surface of the water. From this position, have the swimmers practice rotating up to a vertical standing position (as on deck).

2. In a Crane position in shallow water, practice the Reverse Catalina Rotation, while one partner rolls the vertical leg out and another partner supports and turns the horizontal leg in.

3. Using the correct sculling techniques, practice the Reverse Catalina Rotation facing the wall in a Crane position with the top of the left foot resting on the gutter.

4. Practice the correct execution away from the wall without partners.

Common Errors	Corrections
• Legs move out of their respective planes as the Rotation begins	• Rotate or twist the knees of both legs to rotate the hips. Piking during the Rotation will also cause the legs to go out of alignment.
• Piking into the side Crane position.	• Press the hips forward into the side Crane position.
• Horizontal leg floats up and pops out of the water when passing through the side Crane.	• Press both legs away from each other while passing through the side Crane and keep rolling or turning the legs (right out, left in).
• Piking or "sitting" toward the end of the Rotation, causing loss of height or hip drop.	• Extend or reach with the big toe of the right leg. Press the hips forward so they feel like they are arching as the body rolls onto the back. Make sure to hold the hips in place while the hands transfer from Support scull to Standard scull. Tighten the buttock of the horizontal leg, and press up toward the surface on the tailbone.
• Body rotates into an Aurora position.	• After the body reaches the side Crane position, begin moving the right shoulder toward the surface and bend slightly in at the waist.
• Ballet leg comes over the face on the rise at the completion of the Rotation.	• Keep pressing the hips forward by tightening the left buttock. Press the right leg away from the face. Release pressure of the horizontal leg toward the bottom after the body rolls onto the back.

(Cont.)

Common Errors (cont.)

- Popping out at the end of the Rotation during the surfacing sequence.

- Grabbing at the water as the face surfaces.

Corrections (cont.)

- Slow the upward momentum just beneath the surface by pressing back on the head, neck, and shoulders. Scull softer and deeper. Use the scull only to keep the hips supported after the arm change. Apply stretch to lift the leg while holding the chest down.

- Slow the momentum of the surfacing action and scull at an even pace with just the forearm and wrist. Isolate the shoulders and upper arms from the lower-arm movement.

Chapter 5: Vertical Rotations

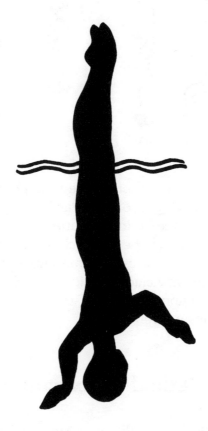

Vertical Rotations comprise an integral part of many synchronized swimming figures. They are generally executed in one of two ways—either slowly at a constant water level as in the Twist, or in a descending uniform motion as in the Spin. Some figures, like the Albatross, include a Half Twist; others, such as the Nova, require a Full Twist. A Spin added at the end of many figures increases the degree of difficulty assigned to that figure. Twists also can be added to the end of some figures to increase the degree of difficulty.

This section will cover the first Vertical Rotations that should be taught to swimmers. As their skill level increases, their ability to execute the Twists and Spins will increase. For this level of swimmer, the Half Twist, the Twirl, and the 180 Degree Spin will be introduced and taught. The next volume, *Coaching Advanced Synchronized Swimming Effectively*, will include the remaining Twists and Spins required for any kind of competition.

Half Twist

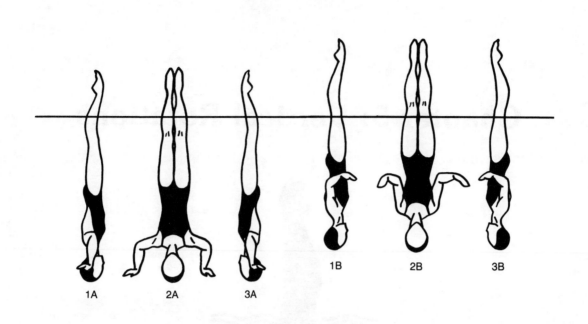

1A   2A   3A   1B   2B   3B

Adding a Half Twist to the end of some of the figures usually increases the degree of difficulty by .1. The swimmer must learn to control a Half Twist at maximum height before attempting a Full Twist. Some figures, such as the Albatross and the Knight include a Half Twist as part of the execution of the figure. The body is not always in an Inverted Vertical position; some figures require a Crane or Bent Knee Vertical position. It is important that the swimmer learn the correct techniques and concepts presented here so that she can transfer this knowledge to other figures and/or hybrids that include a Half Twist.

Method of Execution

The Half Twist is a rotation of the body in an Inverted Vertical position of 180 degrees. The twist should be performed slowly and controlled at a speed consistent with the rest of the figure. The entire Twist is performed at the same water level. In order to perform the Half Twist, the swimmer must be able to hold a Vertical and descend with a degree of control that will allow her to stop and hold the Vertical at an established water line.

The Vertical

To begin, the swimmer should assume an Inverted Vertical position. After the swimmer finds a natural floating point, have her hold still and then execute a Vertical Descent (refer to pp. 53-55 for a review, if necessary). When first learning this skill, especially before a Support scull has been mastered, the arms should be in an overhead Torpedo scull position. The swimmer can progress to a Support scull as she acquires more strength and body control.

Next, have the swimmers descend from the height of the Vertical and establish the same water level. They should hold the Vertical and then submerge. During these stages, the coach and swimmer will constantly check the body position for a good straight Vertical from the front as well as the back. Any uneven-ness of the body will cause the Twist to tilt and/or travel.

The Twist

Bend the elbows so the hands are even with the ears. Use an even, very wide Torpedo scull (sometimes referred to as a "totem pole" position). The swimmer should think about turning in the direction of left side backward, right side forward. The sculls will become un-matched as the left hand makes a larger figure eight to *pull* the body around in the Twist. At the completion of the Half Twist, the hands resume an even scull to maintain a strong Vertical before submerging.

If the swimmer is using a Support scull, the sculls will become unmatched as the right hand makes a larger scull outward to *push* the body around in the Twist. The swimmer should press back on the left side of the body and pull forward on the right side to turn.

Teaching Progression

On the Deck Have the Swimmers:

1. Stand in a good Vertical position, with arms overhead as in a Torpedo scull. Have them turn toward the left shoulder to get the feeling of left side back, right side forward.

2. Continue the above exercise, adding the Torpedo scull action. Think about the left hand making a larger figure eight to *pull* the body around.

In the Water Have the Swimmers:

1. Practice the Log Roll (see *Coaching Synchronized Swimming Effectively* page 48-49).

2. Lie on their backs with their toes touching the side of the pool. Using the Torpedo scull, they should execute a Half Twist so their faces end up in the water. Be certain the left shoulder rotates toward the bottom of the pool and the right shoulder rotates up.

3. In shoulder-deep water, assume an In-verted Vertical position with the hands overhead in a Torpedo scull. Have them perform the Half Twist, using the Torpedo scull. Make sure their rotation is toward the left side.

4. In deep water, assume an Inverted Vertical at the natural buoyancy level specific to each swimmer. They should use the Torpedo scull to execute a Half Twist and then finish with a Vertical Descent.

5. In deep water, with feet downward to the bottom of the pool, try doing the Half Twist while moving down. This helps to build strength.

6. Perform the Half Twist and work on pull-ing the hands down closer to the ears (totem pole position) so the arms are at a 90-degree angle. As the swimmers be-come stronger and gain more body con-trol, they should add a Support scull and more height.

Common Errors	Corrections
• Traveling around in a circle or just to the side, forward or back.	• Check the body alignment. Head should be in line with the body, shoulders and hips even, and arms level, with only the size of the sculls being unmatched. It may help to tell swimmers that it feels like they are traveling in the opposite direction of the way they are actually moving.
• Bouncy Vertical, the water line is not consistent.	• Swimmer is too high and does not have the strength to hold the Vertical. The hands may be working unevenly or not hard enough. Sculling the body down to the bottom of the pool can help build arm strength and body control.

Twirl

1A   2A   3A   4A   5A

1B   2B   3B

The Twirl is a rapid rotation executed at the height of the figure. It adds .2 to the degree of difficulty in such figures as Catalinas and Flamingos. Once mastered with control and stability, the Twirl lends itself beautifully to hybrid construction. The swimmer should have a stable and reliable Vertical position before attempting the techniques described here.

Method of Execution

This skill is executed from an Inverted Vertical position with a Support scull. It is a rapid 180-degree rotation executed at the height of the figure. Of the two methods of executing this skill, Number 1 should be learned first, and Number 2 only when the swimmer is very proficient at Support scull and has good body control.

Technique Number One:

From an Inverted Vertical position with Support scull, both hands move on the out scull to a position in which the hands are toward the bottom of the pool at shoulder level, and the elbows are slightly bent. The left hand moves, little finger leading, to a position above the right armpit and near the right shoulder. The movement is in a circular path from the left side to the front and on to the right arm, with the elbow bending some as it moves. Simultaneously, the right hand moves to a position over the left ear near the top of the head. The hand presses back in a circular path to the head. As soon as the arm positions are reached, both arms press to a position overhead to stop movement of the body at a 180-degree turn, palms press-

ing out and up. A vigorous Torpedo scull is then executed with palms toward the bottom to create a pause at the height of the figure, followed by a Vertical Descent, with arms overhead alternating Torpedo and Dolphin sculls to maintain a continuous rate of descent.

Technique Number Two:

In the second method the right arm reaches across the body on the inward portion of the Support scull and pulls the body around 180 degrees as the arm returns to an outward position of scull. The left arm continues to pull the body around on the inward portion of its scull. Support scull is then continued. The elbows should remain close to the sides of the body throughout the Twirl.

Teaching Progression

On the Deck Have the Swimmers:

1. Practice methods one and two with good posture. Practice the arm movements slowly, concentrating on good form.

2. Practice both techniques while gradually speeding up the action until they can be done rapidly. *Note:* The arm action for Technique 2 will be slower in the water than that for Technique 1.

In the Water Have the Swimmers:

Practice both techniques in a submerged, head-up, Vertical position first. Facing the side of the pool, the swimmers should hold the body under with Support scull and practice the Twirl. The left hip and shoulder should press back and the right hip and shoulder forward in order to Twirl in the correct direction. If this does not occur, swimmer is not using the proper arm action to turn the

body. Watch from the front to make sure the arm action is correct. Be sure swimmers hold in their stomachs and avoid arching their hips as they practice. The body should go deeper as the Twirl is executed. Have them practice until they are proficient with their feet pointing down. Next they should practice the Twirl in an Inverted Vertical position with the water level at the ankles. For Technique 1, the arms should begin stretched out to the sides at shoulder level. As the swimmer becomes proficient, she should increase the height until the Twirl is being executed at maximum height in Support scull. If problems occur, have the swimmer return to a lower height and concentrate on the form of the arm action and tightness of the torso. Arching the body and shoulders will be common with Technique 1, and piking the hips will occur with Technique 2.

Common Errors	**Corrections**
• Loss of body alignment.	• Press hips forward and squeeze buttocks. Flatten the stomach and press it toward the spine, with rib cage rolled down and back.
• Turning more or less than 180 degrees.	• Practice looking at walls and adjusting arm action until correct turn is achieved.
• Sinking on Twirl.	• For Technique 1, press up slightly before initiating the arm action. Press up on arm action to correct position overhead. More vigorous Torpedo needed at end of arm action. For Technique 2, hold elbows in and use more vigorous arm action.
• Twirl looks like a twist, too slow.	• For Technique 2, reach farther across the body with the right arm. Pull harder and more rapidly with both arms.

180 Degree Spin

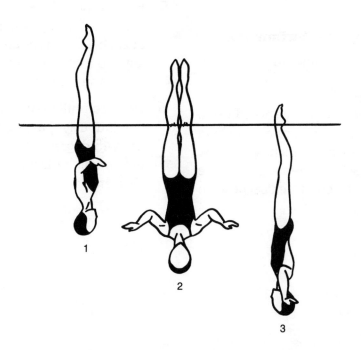

The 180 Degree Spin is the first step in learning to execute the beautiful spins performed by the elite-level swimmers. Once these basics have been mastered, the 360-degree and continuous spins will be easier to teach and execute. A 180 Degree Spin adds .2 to the degree of difficulty of a figure and can make a hybrid very interesting.

Method of Execution

This skill is executed from an Inverted Vertical with Support scull. Swimmers should think of it as doing a Half Twist and a Vertical Descent simultaneously. Beginning at maximum height, the swimmer should ease up slightly on Support scull as the twist begins and continue to ease up on the scull as she turns. The 180 degree rotation should finish as the heels reach the surface of the water. The Vertical Descent is then finished. The swimmer should divide her legs into fourths from her height in Support scull to her heel. One fourth of the leg should descend at each 45 degrees of rotation. This will keep the descent even as the swimmer turns and allow her to be at her heels as she finishes the rotation. The body should turn and descend continuously at a constant speed. The swimmer should press back on the left side of the body and pull forward on the right side to turn.

Teaching Progression

On the Deck Have the Swimmers:

1. Review Support scull and Vertical Descent, maintaining good posture. They should practice again turning the body 180 degrees as they go through descent motions. Note the water level on the legs at each 45 degrees.

In the Water Have the Swimmers:

1. Review the Vertical Descent.

2. Review the Half Twist.

3. Put the two together. They should mark the water levels on their legs by touching each point and reminding themselves how much rotation each level represents. Have them assume an Inverted Vertical position with Support scull and practice Vertical Descent, pausing at each level until they are sure where each one is located.

4. Practice a Half Twist, pausing at each 45 degrees of rotation until they know these points well.

5. Put the Half Twist and Vertical Descent together. Initially, swimmers should pause at each 45 degrees and check their water level to make sure they have descended the correct amount.

6. Practice until they can spin and descend continuously, passing their water levels at each 45 degrees with no pauses. The arm action will be the same as for a Vertical Descent.

Common Errors	**Corrections**
• Descending too rapidly.	• Maintain a stronger Support scull, easing up more gradually.
• Descending too slowly or remaining at a constant level while turning.	• Ease up more on scull. If near buoyancy level, begin to use one of the pull under arm actions sooner.
• Body alignment is off.	• Practice good posture lying on the back on the deck. Stand up and practice posture with a partner. Hang at ankles in an Inverted Vertical. When a good position is attained, lock in and slowly rise to height keeping body locked in position. Try not to move body as the arms move.

Part II: Program Components

Mastering skills is only the first step in building a successful team. After that, the various figures need to be choreographed to music, the team must learn how to stay in shape, and plans must be made for attending meets. Part II presents general information on these subjects that the coach can modify to suit his or her team.

Chapter 6 covers many components that are judged in the choreography of a routine. It also includes factors to consider when choreographing trio and team routines. (How to choreograph for solo and duet routines will be presented in *Coaching Advanced Synchronized Swimming Effectively*). Chapter 7 examines the training concerns of the synchronized swimmer and presents workout plans for the swimmer's total fitness needs. Tips for organizing your team are offered in Chapter 8, including suggestions for planning a yearly workout schedule, considerations for age group programs, and guidelines for planning your first team trip.

Chapter 6: Choreographing Synchronized Swim Routines

Performing synchronized patterns to music through strong and fluid movement is the goal of every coach and performer. In creating a new routine, the coach must carefully consider the components that will be rated by the judges as well as those that will simply enhance the routine's appearance. This chapter offers ways to improve synchronization, achieve fluidity, enhance creativity in movement design, use and interpret music, achieve transitions, and choreograph trio and team routines.

Construction of the Routine

Of the many elements in a synchronized swimming routine, those scored by a judge under Construction of the Routine include Variety, Fluidity, and Creative Action. The following pages present these elements for consideration as the basis for choreographing routines. Construction of the Routine carries 30% weight, the same as that of Synchronization and Difficulty in the trio and team events. (The scoring percentages used in this chapter are from the 1985–86 Official Rules. For current rules, contact your local Technical Chairperson or the Synchro-USA National Office.)

Variety of Music and Movement

Variety, along with fluidity and creative action, constitutes about one-third of the construction grade that is evaluated under the Content score. Nonetheless, it is variety that adds the zest to a routine and transforms it from average to outstanding. When taken to the extreme, however, variety can result in an unsatisfying composition. It should be used cautiously, so that the final routine paints a complete picture rather than a potpourri of movements and positions that lack an overall design.

Like a good story, a routine that "sells," should use the elements of star, chain, and hook. The star is the element that captures the viewer's attention. The chain is the continuity that leads to the hook—the final clincher that grabs the audience and stirs up conversation about the performance. To a great extent, the skillful use of variety can help to achieve this objective.

On examining variety from a *broad* perspective, it becomes apparent that there are at least three elements that can profoundly affect the balance of a routine.

Music Dictates Variety

Music provides the basis for structuring variety. Numerous types of music are available for accompanying synchronized swimming. Routines can be set to jazz, classical, contemporary, ethnic, rock and roll, and so on. Depending on the composition of the music, variety can be achieved by changing tempos or major and minor keys, as well as by using portions of the song played by various instruments. Skillfully used, music can evoke positive responses in the listener and the swimmer. The key purpose of music, however, is to serve as the basis for interpretation in choreography.

Musical variety can be abused when small segments of good music are juxtaposed upon one another, creating an unsatisfying "whole." When in doubt, use segments of no less than one minute, making sure that each separate cut comes to a conclusion and then blends, in key and tempo, into the next. Remember, although music is not a judged factor, it can subliminally influence the judge's opinion of your routine and the audience's reaction to it.

Style and Variety

Style refers to the genre of movement and is directly influenced by music. Stylistic changes can help maintain interest throughout the routine. Because many aesthetic aspects of synchronized swimming resemble dance, style can be changed through varied application of jazz, ballet, modern, or ethnic dance movements. Contrasting slow, lyrical movements with rapid staccato moves can also be effective.

Patterns Provide Variety

Even if swimmers use only one piece of music and a homogeneous style, they can add an important element of variety by including many different patterns in a routine. The simplest routine can become interesting to watch when it features lines, circles, symmetrical, and asymmetrical patterns. A dynamic dimension can be achieved by using patterns that change on the surface rather than consistently using underwater pattern transitions.

An Inventory of Variety

Up to this point, we have discussed variety in general terms. The following specifics may provide a helpful index for analyzing and implementing variety in routines.

- Strokes: breast, side, back, crawl, combinations.

- Propulsion: stroking, sculling, Eggbeater, traveling hybrids, connected patterns that move.

- Arm movements: straight, curved, bent, open hands, closed hands, soft hands, flexed or hyperextended hands, single or double arms.

- Hybrids: Verticals, Splits, hooks, tucks, pikes, Cranes, Herons, Ballet Legs, thrusts, rockets.

- Surfaces: in figures, with arms, scull-ups, push-ups, strokes.

- Patterns: Connected, tight, spread, circles, lines, asymmetrical, symmetrical changes on surface, changes underwater.

- Descents: with arms, vertical drops, tucks, pikes, in tandem, slow, rapid.

Some routines seem to go on endlessly and others leave us wanting more. Obviously, every choreographer wants to achieve the latter, and perhaps no other element can facilitate this objective more than variety.

Fluidity

More difficult to define, but equally important to master is the element of *fluidity*. When working toward varied movements, positions, and music, it is important to be fluid.

In figure scoring, fluidity falls in the Control part of the award under "...a smooth, precise and constant tempo of transitions and positions...." *(United States Synchronized Swimming Official Rules*, p. 32) In routine scoring, fluidity is considered part of the Construction of the Routine.

Swimmers can attain the "constant tempo of transitions and positions" required in figures by counting throughout the execution of the figure. The coach and swimmer should select the number of counts for each figure position and maintain that cadence throughout the performance. For an intermediate swimmer, using 1-1,000, 2-1,000, 3-1,000, 4-1,000 for each position will provide an even speed of action that can be controlled. The beginner may require a faster count and the more advanced swimmer may need a slower count to execute the figure fluidly with control.

Webster defines *fluid* as that which can flow. Flow is further defined as that which moves as a liquid does, or to have smooth and pleasing continuity.

Fluidity in routines is truly "that which moves as a liquid does." The swimmer should seek to have "smooth and pleasing continuity" in the Construction of the Routine. A routine begins and ends with the music. Every action performed within that time period should flow, both above and under water. Smooth, dynamic transitions that flow from one skill to the next guarantee fluid choreography. (A discussion of transitions is included later in this chapter.)

Synchronizing movements to the music and to each other will also improve the flow of the routine. Patterns made above and below the water should appear smooth, precise, and dynamic. The coach and swimmer should avoid jerky, unbalanced, static patterns. The routine should appear as though there is continuous movement throughout.

One way to ensure fluidity in a routine is to make certain the swimmer is strong enough to execute the choreography. A strong kick will aid the swimmer's fluidity while doing arm strokes. Sculling strength will help in the execution of the figures and hybrids.

Creative Action

Creative Action, the third element under the heading Construction of the Routine, is as important as fluidity and variety when choreographing a routine. Although it is difficult to be totally original, the coach and swimmer can achieve creative action by doing something a little differently or putting skills together in a unique way.

A routine that evolves from one's own thoughts or imagination is fun to write, fun to watch, and best of all, fun to swim! The enthusiasm generated in using one's own ideas and the satisfaction felt when others appreciate them will definitely add to the routine's presentation.

Of the many ways to be creative, the use of the music may be the most important. The music alone can tell you what to write—when to start, when to stop, when to turn, when to spin, when to pile up, when to peel off, when to dance, when to float, when to be country, when to be rock and roll, and when to knock the audience off their feet. The music doesn't have to be "far out" or "in," but it helps if it is something you and your swimmers can enjoy and relate to. If you like it, you will enjoy working with it! It also helps to choose different music each year or for each new routine you write so that you have a fresher outlook to new and different ideas. A variety of music and rhythms gives your writing some depth. Double counting the music can add a whole different dimension. A slow 4 count followed by a quick 8 or 16 count can change the pace and style of the arrangement considerably. Music with words, repetitions, or sounds can also be used. The swimmers can do what the words say or peel off individually or into fours and fours as the melody repeats.

The most basic idea can become a creative movement when put to the right piece of music as shown by the following team's efforts to choreograph a routine to a tango medley. After trying many ways to make a Dolphin Chain original, the team decided to listen to the music again, this time more critically. The music began slow, paused, and then sped up faster and faster with a turning sound. The swimmers hooked up into fours for a Dolphin Chain. The first and fourth swimmers led down to form two pinwheels. As the music turned, they rotated—not head or foot-first, but sideways, pivoting at the top. The music made it an exciting, unique routine.

Creative action can also be a part of stroking and hybrids. Almost anything you can think of and are willing to try can get you results! Be creative and try these experiments:

- Reverse strokes forward to backward.

- Use a head, shoulder, or body move between the arm motion and kick.

- Hook up to do a double or group stroke or hybrid.

- Execute an arm and leg move together— one swimmer using the arm, the other swimmer using the leg.

- Face different directions to start a hybrid and stop at the same wall to finish.

- Hold the same arm pose at different levels.

- Add character with facial expressions.

- Clap the hands, kick the feet, splash, snap the fingers, flex the feet, or even scull to the music.

- Do an unexpected ending in your hybrid—for example, a Chain Dolphin started on the back and finished on the stomach.

- Use the wall, the gutter of the pool, or each other for support during a hybrid, arm, or leg move.

Pool patterns are another area in which to be creative. For example, an ordinary pattern change done with the head up while stroking or sculling can become unique if it is performed with the head down and the legs up in a Vertical position. Combining surface and underwater changes also adds interest. Swimming into a corner of the pool and back out or down the side is an unusual movement. Or have the swimmers cross in front of or behind each other, moving in and out, or in opposite ways (clockwise and counter-clockwise, right to left, left to right).

Creativity can begin on the deck. A swimmer can roll, flip, dance, or even dive over someone into the pool. Although these land motions are not judged, they usually set the stage and thus should immediately capture the spectators' and judges' attention. Well written deckwork offers another advantage; a swimmer who hears immediate applause will be that much more motivated throughout the rest of her routine.

Plan your floats and lifts creatively as well. A float can add beauty and a change of pace, and a lift can add strength, difficulty, and a risk factor. These movements are unique because they require more than one person and can be varied in so many ways. Floats can be constructed on land and then put into the water. They can be performed with the face up or down, while the swimmers are turning, stationary, or traveling, or even underwater. Lifts can be done by partners or a group, with head up or under, or with the swimmer held stable or boosted high out of the water.

It takes a great deal of time to develop creative action of any kind. The following tips may help you speed up the process.

- Get ideas from such special events as cheerleading, gymnastics, ice dancing, marching bands, figure skating, aerobic dance exercise classes, ballet, theatrical shows or musicals, television music or dance programs, ice shows, or videos.

- Start with a basic routine and let the music create the mood and sell your idea.

- Don't look at anything only once; give the idea time to develop.

- Let your strongest swimmer test the ideas.

- If you get stuck on one part, go on to something else and come back to it later.

- Play the music over and over again while your swimmers are executing whatever comes to their minds in the water. Pick and choose the actions that go with the music and that also can be cleanly executed by all of the swimmers involved.

It takes courage to be different and hard work to be imaginative, but the results are well worth the effort. Originality will enlighten the audience, add to the fun for you and your swimmers, and maybe even captivate a judge or two!

Closely related to Creative Action but judged separately is the Use and Interpretation of the Music. The choreography should not only be creative and original but also reflect the music through the swimmer's use and interpretation.

Use and Interpretation of the Music

Although Use and Interpretation of the Music accounts for only 10% of the Content score, it ranks as an important element in the routine score. In fact, this element is the very essence of synchronized swimming because it affects all the other components of the routine.

Selecting the Music

When selecting the music, consider using a *subtle* theme—that is, a single strand or idea that runs through several pieces of music that are "cut" together. Although not required, a theme can add interest and cohesion to a routine. For example, a nautical theme for a younger team might include "Anchors Aweigh," "Yellow Submarine," "Surfin' USA," and "Popeye."

The music should demonstrate contrast, and yet the pieces must be compatible. This can be achieved by selecting pieces with different musical qualities and cutting them carefully and in a logical order.

Include a variety of music—slow, flowing, dramatic, powerful, lively, and fast. Although all types of music are acceptable—from classical to show tunes to rock—remember to make your program pleasing to the ears of the audience and the judges.

The routine must be choreographed to fit the music, with the movements following the tempo of the music. For example, the choreography should flow when the music does, be crisp when the music indicates crisp-ness, and be dramatic or funny along with the music. Strokes should be related to the type of music. Gimmicks are great when used sparingly and performed well. Accent the highs in the music with high lifts, pop-ups, and rockets. Special effects in the music, such as bells, gongs and cymbals, are great for accenting movements. Facial movements can also help in the interpretation of the selected music. Showing emotion through looks of surprise, fun, anger, and so on add to the use and interpretation of the music and can be an especially strong element in a solo.

If the swimmer were to perform the routine without the music, the choreography should reflect the essence of the music. The spectator should be able to sense the music because of the swimmer's choreographic use and interpretation.

No matter how well you have used the music or how creative, fluid, or varied your routine is, it will not look like it belongs in the sport of synchronized swimming unless all of the swimmers are performing alike. The next section, coaching synchronization, will help you achieve that goal.

Coaching Synchronization

The word *synchronized* distinguishes this sport from all other aquatic disciplines. Synchronization is the essence of synchronized swimming because nothing is as detrimental to a routine as a performance that is not in unison. The layperson generally evaluates the proficiency of a team, trio, or duet by its synchronization. Even the highly trained eye may fail to appreciate good choreography and superior execution when they are obscured by poor synchronization. Although synchronization constitutes only 30% of the Content score, the coach should consider this element to be fundamental to the success of any routine.

Unlike execution, which can be limited by the developmental level of the swimmer, all swimmers can reach a high level of proficiency in synchronization if the following two considerations are strictly observed: The Basic Criteria for Establishing Synchronization and the Teaching Sequence.

Basic Criteria for Establishing Synchronization

The first criterion is that the choreography must be commensurate with the skill level of the swimmers. Using movements that are too fast or too awkward, or that demand more strength than the swimmers have will inevitably result in poor synchronization.

Use arm and leg positions that can be executed uniformly. To some extent, the complexity of these positions will be determined by skill level. However, many positions are simply impossible to unify and should be avoided. Let your *eye* determine what to avoid, for synchronization is as dependent upon uniform *placement* as it is upon *movement* to tempo.

Synchronization involves two essential factors—the static factor (position) and the dynamic factor (movement). Steps in teaching synchronization should address these two aspects of synchronization.

Teaching Sequence

The following are the sequential steps in the instructional phases for achieving synchronization.

1. *Establish the preliminary choreography.* This is best accomplished in the water to ensure that movements and positions look good and are compatible with the swimmer(s).

2. *Set counts for every aspect of the choreography.* This should include such details as counts for water levels on descents, surfacing counts, and underwater work. The counts should be precise enough so that the swimmers know them without using the music.

3. *Set the positions in land drill.* Every move and every position should be precisely set. Although initially a very time consuming process, it will save an infinite amount of time and yield positive results in the long run.

4. *Have repetitive practice on routine sequences in the water.* Begin this once the static (positions) and dynamic (movement) aspects of the routine have been clearly defined.

Methodology

The *methods* used during the initial learning of the routine and throughout the fine-tuning process can have a profound effect on the ultimate success. The coach should use teaching methods that are comfortable and reflect his or her style. The following methods may prove helpful.

- *Begin with a slow tempo* and gradually increase it as muscle memory steadily improves. Remember, it may be counterproductive to insist on endurance before movements are internalized.

- At every stage, *insist upon perfection of position.* By doing this, you are actually coaching execution as well as synchronization.

- *Use only a fraction of each count.* Obviously, there is much room for poor synchronization within one count. Ideally, each movement should be so precisely defined that it could be likened to an individual snapshot.

The job of coaching synchronization can seem overwhelming if one considers that a five-minute routine has literally hundreds of counts and that each count provides the opportunity for eight synchronization errors in a team of eight swimmers. Fortunately, good synchronization can be achieved with patience and perseverance and can dramatically improve the final product. Once your routine is synchronized, working on transitions will help smooth out any rough spots in the choreography.

Transitions

A transition is the movement, or movements, required to change from one position to another. This change can be performed within a figure, from a horizontal position to a vertical position and vice versa, and from a figure to a stroke and vice versa.

Some key points to remember when executing any kind of transition are:

- Each action must be smooth and fluid.

- The swimmer should demonstrate ease during the execution.

- The transition should be executed in a logical progression.

When changing positions within a figure, the movement should also be constant and evenly paced. Counting or using the metronome during the various phases of the figure will help the swimmer establish a rhythmical pattern to the performance. Unless specifically noted in the rules, there should be no traveling during figure competition. This problem can usually be corrected by making sure the swimmer has her hands at the correct angle and proper body alignment. The swimmer should learn to use the muscles in the body rather than the hands during the figure transitions.

Traveling while executing a figure or hybrid during a routine is encouraged and adds fluidity to the choreography. Changing from a horizontal position to a vertical one requires a show of strength, fluidity, and effortless execution. Less experienced swimmers tend to make an abrupt stop or an awkward movement as they switch their horizontal momentum to vertical.

When horizontal, the swimmer is usually either on her back or stomach prior to a change into a vertical position. If she is on her stomach, face downward, the swimmer should bend and tuck both knees under the body. Lifting the body vertically upward from the trunk, she begins the Eggbeater kick immediately. Adding arm movements usually helps to speed up the vertical lift. To vary this transition, the swimmer should try extending one leg sideward as the other one is tucked under the body, beginning the Eggbeater kick as the trunk is lifted upward. Be creative and have the swimmers try new ways of getting their legs under the body for the horizontal to vertical transition.

From a horizontal position on the back, face upward, the swimmer should bend one knee as the lower back is arched. Sculling toward the feet, she presses the other leg toward the bottom of the pool and begins the Eggbeater kick immediately. To vary this transition, have the swimmer kick the leg up out of the water instead of bending the knee. Simultaneously, she should bend and drop the other leg toward the bottom of the pool, beginning the Eggbeater.

To attain height throughout these transitions, the swimmer must begin the Eggbeater kick as soon as possible while the vertical position is being established. Failure to do so results in a drop in height and an awkward movement.

When moving from a vertical to a horizontal position, either on the back or stomach, the swimmer should maintain a kicking action throughout the transition. From the Eggbeater kick, one breast stroke kick into the flutter kick will provide the impetus for the desired forward motion. If this seems too awkward, the swimmer should move one leg toward the surface of the water maintaining the Eggbeater kick. As the head and trunk are lowered to the surface, the other leg should also move toward the surface. The kick should change to a flutter kick on the side, back or stomach. If the body drops in height, it is usually because the swimmer is not maintaining either an Eggbeater or flutter kick throughout the transition.

While performing a routine, a swimmer frequently strokes into a figure or hybrid. Remember, the choreography must continue its movement in a fluid fashion. If the figure or hybrid begins in a Back Layout position, some kind of back stroke or side stroke roll to the back movement is most often used. From a Front Layout position, a breast stroke, crawl stroke, side stroke, or combination of any of these will help the swimmer flow into the figure or hybrid. Once the swimmer and coach understand how to maintain the fluid forward movement, any creative arm stroke can be choreographed into a figure or hybrid. The coach should make sure the swimmer does not stop the forward motion and "get ready" to execute the figure or hybrid. This transition, like the others, should be smooth and logical and appear easy to execute.

If a figure or hybrid is completed at the surface of the water in a Front or Back Layout position, the transition to a vertical position will be the same as that for changing from a horizontal to a vertical position, which was covered above. The swimmer also has the option of stroking while in the horizontal position instead of lifting to the vertical. Whatever transition is employed, the coach should make sure that it is smooth, fluid, and logical.

Many figures and hybrids finish underwater. There are several ways the swimmer can return to the surface. However, the swimmer must be careful not to ascend in the same hole through which she descended. Moving underwater helps the swimmer to achieve pool coverage and also adds an element of surprise to the choreography. Have the swimmers try the following ways of returning to the surface.

- In what is sometimes called a pop-up, the swimmer rises headfirst to the surface, strives for maximum height, and then sinks. A strong Eggbeater kick is used, followed by a powerful breast stroke kick. The body should be tucked somewhat—bent at the waist, shoulders rounded, and the chin tucked down on the chest. The upper body straightens as the body emerges from the water. The swimmer can choose whether or not to use arm movements.

- Executing the pop-up described above, the swimmer maintains the height instead of sinking. She holds her body above the water with an Eggbeater kick. Once again, arm movement is optional.

- The swimmer should surface footfirst, arch her body, and Torpedo scull onto her back. If she wants to achieve a vertical position, have her follow the instructions on page 85 for changing from a horizontal to a vertical position.

- Have the swimmers surface footfirst and pike, using a Lobster scull, into a Front Layout position. They can then use the horizontal to vertical transition.

- Another option is for the swimmer to surface footfirst into a Split position and then execute a Walkout to a Back Layout. To vary this, the swimmer can move the same arm and leg over the surface of the water.

- Using a flutter kick diagonally toward the surface from the Vertical Descent, the swimmer can rise on the side, front, or back of the body. Almost any kind of arm movement can be used as the swimmer surfaces.

At this point, the swimmer and coach are limited only by their own creativity. Remember to think about variety when evaluating the contents of the routine, so that you don't keep repeating the same transitions.

Applying Dance Techniques to Synchronized Swimming

The sport of synchronized swimming is often compared to dance, gymnastics (floor exercise), and figure skating. This comparison is made because these activities use movements like those that synchro participants do in the water.

These three sister sports—gymnastics, figure skating, and synchro—share various characteristics. The aesthetic quality of movement ranks as the most outstanding shared characteristic and the one that gives these sports so much spectator appeal. The general spectator is easily drawn into the performance of a single gymnast in a floor exercise routine or the energy of the figure skating pair, or the dynamics of an eight-swimmer routine of a synchro team.

Like dancers, synchronized swimmers move in specific directions, to specific beats, using their own manner of presentation. What distinguishes synchro from many other sports is its purpose, which is to perform. A synchro swimmer is working toward a goal that cannot be evaluated by space, weight, or time. A synchro performance cannot be measured in the fixed and objective forms of measurement used in basketball, hockey, tennis, or track events. Synchronized swimming, figure skating, gymnastics, and dance are subjective, and the performance outcome is determined solely by the performance itself. No equipment is needed.

To excel in synchronized swimming, the swimmer needs more than excellence in executing figures, security of strength, and the full range of movement with flexibility. Like dancers, synchronized swimmers need to exhibit pizazz—showmanship—moxie—ham—sparkle. Whatever the name, this quality of aesthetic performance jumps out and reaches the spectators and judges. And when it is missing, we witness a "good" but not dazzling performance.

The following section offers some ways to develop the aesthetic performance in synchronized swimmers. The use of dance techniques figures prominently in improving the overall performance of swimmers in both routines and figures.

Use sharp music with a 4/4 or 2/4 beat to accompany these exercises.

Head Position

"The head position determines the movement and position of the entire body." This quote, well known among dancers and gymnasts, should be heard more often in synchro. A tucked chin or arched head can ruin the straightest of all lines within the body line. Coaches need to work industriously with their swimmers on the use, posture, and angle of the head.

Head Movement Exercises

On Deck Have the Swimmers:

Sit cross-legged (Indian fashion) with their back very flat (vertical). To correct a rounded back, place the outside of your lower leg against the swimmer's lower back with the outside of your ankle at the base of her spine. Pull her shoulders back toward your knee while maintaining the vertical alignment of your lower leg against her back. The back must be vertical. Put your palms over the swimmer's ears. With your fingers pointing down gently pull her neck *long*. As you look down at the swimmer, you can see vertical alignment. Most people have a "forward" head. This small pull upward and out will lengthen the line of the neck. In synchronized swimming, high chins and the appearance of long necks are desirable.

Exercise Number 1:   Begin in a sitting position with the head forward. Execute each move on one count for an eight-count exercise set.

   Count 1:   Look up, reaching upward with the chin.

   Count 2:   Head forward.

   Count 3:   Look down, putting the chin on the chest.

Count 4: Head forward.

Count 5: Tilt the head to the right; reach the left ear up.

Count 6: Head forward.

Count 7: Tilt the head to the left; reach the right ear up.

Count 8: Head forward.

Add head turns to the right and left, making sure the swimmers keep the chin lifted as the turn is executed. People tend to drop the chin on head turns—a habit that should be avoided.

Note: In most team, trio, and duet work, the counts are sharp. The movement should match the dynamics of the music. Sharp, snappy head movements are a must. Make the movement crisp, on count, abrupt and clean with no after movement.

Exercise Number 2: Sometimes called *rolls*, this movement consists of head swings done in a sitting position. Basically, the head moves like a pendulum—down and to the right, then down and to the left. This movement is often seen in video dances and other contemporary dance. The count is usually *and* for the downward movement (preparation move) and *one* to the side tilt. The face focus remains forward. The movement is executed for eight counts.

Exercise Number 3: Swimmers sit across from a partner for a mirror image. Using short counts, such as 1-2-3-4, one partner executes some head movements. The other partner must repeat those exact movements.

Throughout these deck exercises, the coach should clap and/or count the rhythm at first.

Add music as soon as possible so that the swimmers can learn to move to it. Choose music with a steady 4/4 or 2/4 rhythm that is easily counted.

In the Water Have the Swimmers:

Dress up the Eggbeater lengths by adding some snappy head movements. All of the head movements executed on land can be performed in the water. The head shows more in the water because, except when the arms are up, it is the only part of the body seen above the water in an Eggbeater kick.

Exercise Number 1:

A. Execute a side Eggbeater for eight counts with the trailing arm extended.

B. Do a side Eggbeater for eight counts with a head movement.

C. Press upward to change from side to front Eggbeater with both arms extended forward on the water, palms up or down.

D. Execute a front Eggbeater for eight counts.

E. Execute a front Eggbeater for eight counts using head movements that are different from those done during the side Eggbeater.

F. Press upward to the other side.

G. Repeat the movements.

All of these movements can be modified or rearranged to achieve different accents, counts, and movements. Ask the swimmers to create their own eight-count sets to coincide with specific directions on the Eggbeaters. Insist that they repeat the same eight counts to develop choreographic skills and perfect their movement.

Focus

"Where are you looking?" Nearsighted swimmers cannot see the eyes of the judge 20 feet away. Actually the swimmers only need to see the body sitting in the chair. The important thing is that they focus on a *place* and *spot* and look at it and see it. Many new swimmers give the "blank stare" expression that makes them look as if they are out to lunch or in another world. This happens because they are involved in *counting* and/or performing correctly. Have the swimmers begin focusing early in their routine performance by looking at the judges and spectators. Have them smile. Expression with a head tilt, a chin lift, or eye contact helps communicate the swimmer's confidence, projection, and enjoyment to the judge and audience. Focus is also used in figure competition. When the swimmer swims out to execute the figure she should look at the announcer and the center judge to line herself up.

Arm Work

"What do I do with all that time? It has to be arm moves! I can't do arm strokes or movements! I keep doing the same arm moves!" All of these cries of frustration sound familiar to the seasoned coach. Little does the swimmer know she is capable of doing arm movements and only needs to be guided in the right direction.

Coaches do not need expert training and years of dance lessons to get their swimmers moving their arms. They do not even need to demonstrate. The help that is needed comes from music and mirrors. If mirrors are impossible, go with just the music.

The objectives of working with the arms are (a) to develop fluid arm movements, (b) to provide an opportunity for interpreting the music using only the arms and head, (c) to develop arm, shoulder, and back strength and flexibility, and (d) to increase the variety of movement and the creative use of the arms in the water.

Arm Movement Exercises

On Deck Have the Swimmers:

Sit cross-legged (Indian fashion) with very flat vertical backs. Isolating the legs forces the swimmers to use their upper torso for extension, twisting, and other movements. Keep reminding the swimmers to lift up in the ribs and press down and back on the shoulders. To correct a hunch, have the swimmer lift her shoulders (hunch them) up to a point slightly behind her ears, and hold that position while pressing down on the shoulders. If the position is still not flat, tell her to pinch her shoulder blades together slightly. No matter what, the swimmer must begin with flat shoulders. Doing this arm work with hunched and rounded backs is pointless and a waste of valuable time. If done correctly, arms and shoulders will definitely be tired at the end of a three-minute continuous arm workout done with the shoulders flat and the back vertical.

Exercise Number 1: Using Eight counts, begin with both arms forward, parallel to the ground with palms facing downward.

Count 1:   Put the right hand to the right shoulder. The elbow should be pointing out above the armpit.

Count 2:   Extend the right arm out to the side at shoulder height.

Count 3:   Put the left hand to the left shoulder. The elbow should be pointing out above the armpit.

Count 4:   Extend the left arm out to the side at shoulder height.

Count 5:   Bend the right elbow and put the right hand to the right shoulder.

Count 6:   Extend the right arm forward to the beginning position.

Count 7:   Bend the left elbow and put the left hand to the left shoulder.

Count 8:   Extend the left arm forward to the beginning position.

Exercise Number 2:   Using eight counts, begin with both arms extended to the side, parallel to the ground with the palms up.

Count 1:   Bend the right arm into a 90-degree angle, palm toward the head. Keep the upper arm parallel to the ground.

Count 2:   Move the right arm up into half of a "V" position.

Count 3:   Bend the left arm into a 90-degree angle, with the palm toward the head and the upper arm parallel to the ground.

Count 4:   Move the left arm up into the other half of the "V" position.

Count 5:   Bend the right arm into a 90-degree angle as in Count 1.

Count 6:   Move the right arm out to the beginning position.

Count 7:   Bend the left arm into a 90-degree angle as in Count 3.

Count 8:   Move the left arm out to the beginning position.

These are examples of very clean, simple, sharp arm movements. Try combining the two sets of eight counts to challenge the swimmers. To add diversity, initiate creativity and keep the interest high, have the swimmers sit facing a partner, or mirror image. Using either two or four counts at a time, they should repeat their partner's movements. For example, Sue moves four counts, and Holly repeats the same exact four counts. Sue continues to lead, Holly repeats Sue's movements until the coach says switch.

Exercise Number 3:   For the head, arms, and wrists, begin with both arms extended sideward with palms down, using eight counts for each arm.

Count 1:   Bend the right arm into a 90-degree angle, palm facing forward and hand in an open paw.

Count 2:   Flex the wrist down and tuck the chin, keeping the arm in the 90-degree angle.

Count 3:   Extend the wrist with the hand still in the open paw, head up.

Count 4:   Extend the right arm up into half a "V" position and lift the chin up.

Count 5:   Return to the position in Count 1.

Count 6:   Flex the wrist down and tuck the chin, keeping the arm in the 90-degree angle.

Count 7:   Return to the position in Count 1.

Count 8:   Return the right arm out to the side. Repeat the sequence with the left arm and then with both arms simultaneously.

This exercise offers a real challenge in the water while moving forward. It can also be adapted to the side Eggbeater. Use the right arm when moving toward the left side, both arms when moving forward, and left arm when moving to the right side.

Exercise Number 4: For music improvisation on deck, have the swimmers sit facing a partner for a mirror image. One partner should do arm movements for a specified number of counts (two, four, six, eight). The other partner will follow. Switch so that each swimmer has a chance to be a leader and a follower. Pair a newer swimmer with a more experienced one to share the learning. This will help the newer swimmer feel less inhibited.

As the swimmers gain confidence, they can perform more of these arm movement exercises in the water. Organize the exercises as you would on deck, using pairs in the mirror-image fashion. The partners can do an Eggbeater sideward for the length or width of the pool with one leading and then do an Eggbeater facing the opposite side with the other partner leading. To work a forward Eggbeater, one partner will follow the other halfway down the pool, where both swimmers turn 180 degrees and return with the other partner leading.

Remember to use music as much as possible and choose selections with an expressive beat. Avoid counting so you are able to coach. When a swimmer has trouble thinking of new moves, suggest a change in focus, direction, angle, rhythm, or dynamics, or add head movements.

Leg Work

Serious dancers can compare their leg strength and jumping ability with that of the top basketball and volleyball players. Seldom is a dancer seen working the weight machine. Instead dancers jump continuously in stylized positions, holding bent-knee positions and extending and lifting their legs repeatedly.

Synchronized swimmers do leg work for three reasons: (a) to gain the strength needed to hold a position for a given period of time and raise the body sharply and high out of the water, (b) to achieve flexibility for full-body extension, including the ankles and toes, and for wide splits on top of the water, and (c) to improve leg coordination.

Leg Movement Exercises

Exercise Number 1: "Brushes" for strength are basic movements in ballet and modern dance and are done in most dance classes. Have the swimmers stand with one side to the wall. They should place the hand nearest to the wall on the wall, with palm flat and fingers pointing upward. This arm is extended with the elbow slightly bent. The back should be flat, and the shoulders down and flat. The swimmers should extend their free arm out to the side or forward (rounded at chest height).

Leg movement is done from the hip joint with the stomach held in. The buttocks should be tucked under and the hips remain level. There is no visible movement from the waist down, just steady static contraction. The swimmers should not turn out or twist the leg and hip while executing these exercises. Standing with their feet parallel, pointing forward, they should lead with the front of the thigh on forward brushes, pointing the foot as the leg moves. The side of the thigh leads the side brushes. Backward brushes are led with the back of the knee, and the foot points a little later. The sequence of brushes with the left side toward the wall are:

Counts 1-2:   Put the right leg forward at a low height. The toe touches the deck in point.

Counts 3-4:   Return the leg to the starting position.

Counts 5-6:   Move the right leg to the side at low height. The toe touches the deck in point.

Counts 7-8:   Return leg to starting position.

Counts 1-2:   Move the right leg back at low height. The toe touches the deck in point.

Counts 3-4:   Return the leg to the starting position.

Counts 5-6:   Move the right leg to the side at low height. The toe touches the deck in point.

Counts 7-8:   Return the leg to the starting position.

Have the swimmers turn toward the wall, change hands, and assume the correct starting position. Use only two counts to make this switch. The swimmer should work on the following exercise.

• Repeat the same sequence with the left leg, turn and change.

• Repeat the same sequence at medium height (foot about 12 inches off the floor), turn and change. Use both the right and the left legs.

• Repeat the sequence with the leg height parallel to the deck, right and left legs, turn and change.

On side brushes, the swimmers should allow the leg to rotate (knee pointing up) and turn out in order to reach the horizontal position. In addition, they should avoid any turning out or twisting on backward brushes. Allowing the swimmers to arch their upper torso very slightly forward on each brush will help them achieve this position.

Exercise Number 2:   Standing wall leg lifts will also help swimmers develop Ballet Leg strength. Have them begin with their back to the wall and their heels approximately 2 to 3 inches away from the wall. They should place their hands and arms on the wall in the proper sculling position. The stomach should be pulled in and flattened and the lower back pressed against the wall. They must keep their back flat and their stomach pulled in throughout this exercise.

A. Straight leg lifts with feet parallel are repeated for the right and the left leg.

Counts 1-2-3:   Lift the leg forward and 12 inches off the deck.

Counts 4-5-6-7: Hold the position.

Count 8:   Close the leg down.

Counts 1-2-3:   Lift the leg forward and parallel to the deck.

Counts 4-5-6-7: Hold the position.

Count 8:   Close the leg down.

B. Repeat bent-knee leg lifts for both legs.

Counts 1-2:   Bend leg to the Bent-Knee position.

Counts 3-4:   Extend the leg to the Ballet Leg position, parallel to the floor.

Count 5:   Return to the Bent Knee position.

Count 6:   Extend to the Ballet Leg position.

Count 7:   Return to the Bent Knee position.

Count 8:   Extend to the Ballet Leg position.

Count 1-2-3-4: Hold in the extended Ballet Leg.

Count 5-6:   Return to the Bent Knee position.

Count 7-8:   Return to the starting position.

Watch swimmers carefully for incorrect back positions; correct this problem quickly or stop the swimmer to avoid lower back strain in weaker swimmers. If they are having trouble executing Ballet Legs in the water, these exercises will help develop the leg, hip, stomach, and buttocks muscle groups.

Leg and Foot Flexibility

This subject is covered in the section on Flexibility on pages 103 to 109.

Creative Leg Work on Deck

Apply the process used for arm work to leg work on deck. Have the swimmers pair up and mirror-image leg work with music. (For example, one partner leads with four-count moves, and the other follows.) The object is to keep the heels off the ground for one minute, which can be very exhausting. The following example is an eight-count Ballet Leg sequence, beginning on the back with the upper body supported on the elbows, the stomach in, and the heels off the floor.

Count 1:   Right Bent Knee

Count 2:   Right Ballet Leg

Count 3:   Left Bent Knee (Flamingo position)

Count 4:   Double Ballet Leg position

Count 5:   Right Bent Knee (Flamingo position)

Count 6:   Extend the right leg horizontally.

Count 7:   Left Bent Knee

Count 8:   Extend the left leg into the starting position.

To make sure everyone keeps their legs off the deck, have the swimmers turn around so that they are sitting on the edge of the pool with their elbows on the deck and their legs extended out over the water. It works! Again, vary the type of the music used. Try slow flowing music and stronger, sharp music.

Throughout any of the dance-type leg and arm moves, the coach should continue to correct basic body positions, making sure the head is aligned, the chin high, the shoulders are down and flat, the back is flat, the stomach tucked in and flat, and the buttocks under. When working with the legs, there is a little additional body movement. When the arms move however, the added twist of the upper torso and the slight tilt of the chin can make the difference between a blank "statue-look" and a truly expressive move.

Trio Choreography

Trios were introduced to national synchronized swimming competition in 1984, though the event has been an important element in collegiate competition for many years. Routines must be choreographed specifically for trios, not for a duet plus one or for a team of four minus one. The following section outlines the special elements to consider for effective choreography of a trio.

Selecting the right swimmers for a trio should be your first concern. Try to match up three swimmers who are about the same age and have similar skill levels, strengths, styles, and appearances. Although matching three individuals perfectly in each category is ideal, all combinations should be considered.

Trios work well for those clubs with an uneven number of athletes. In addition, a trio is a viable option for swimmers who are not ready to or do not want to swim a solo.

Selecting music is the next step. All the trio members should assist the coach in the selection, especially if they have had prior experience with choreography. The music should have an identifiable beat and be easy to count. Remember, the swimmers should enjoy the music, so that they will perform well and put their personalities into their presentations. Select music that will stay fresh throughout the season, so that the swimmers do not get bored and lose their feel for it. The composition of a routine should exhibit several moods. Make sure the three swimmers can relate to the moods each piece of music reflects.

While putting the pieces of music together, imagine the routine being broken down into three distinct sections. The first section, the introduction, includes the deckwork and the first lap of the pool. This section sets the stage for the rest of the routine, whether one or more selections of music are used. The main body of the routine makes up the second section, which should continue the action, present various moods, and prepare the audience for the ending. The final section, the ending, should present a climactic conclusion to the routine.

The pieces of music should blend into one another throughout, even if the tempo, mood, and character change totally. Avoid awkward musical transitions (pieces of music that do not fit well together) because they will make the routine much more difficult to choreograph. If there are any clumsy transitions, make the music changes *before* choreographing the routine.

Keep in mind that there are three performers and three distinct parts, when choreographing the routine on land. This factor will lend both a symmetrical and asymmetrical quality to the routine. A proper proportion in the arrangement of two parts using the third as the center will help give the asymmetrical appearance. You can also develop more intricate connecting hybrids that can be exaggerated and create additional space and dimensions. The trio can also add new dimensions by creating lifts. More airborne weight, more variety, and greater risk factors can be achieved. In addition the trio has an advantage in that they can perform peel-offs, in which one swimmer executes a move, followed by the second, and then the third, and add-ons, in which the first swimmer initiates a series of moves that are executed by the second swimmer and then by the third.

All of the special elements discussed here can and should be used to their fullest extent, especially while blending the athletes' particular strengths and styles. Accentuate the best points of the swimmers and choreograph the routine to match their capabilities. You could, for example, increase the interaction of the swimmers in spots where the music demands some humor or drama.

Pool patterns should not present a problem for a trio if the threesome has good fluid movement throughout the routine and covers the pool adequately. Each movement should begin in a different spot from where the previous action was completed. There are only a limited number of patterns a trio can do among themselves. This will be a minor factor, however, if the swimmers show good movement from one pattern to the next and do not hold one pattern too long. Make sure the patterns do not look like a duet using one extra swimmer. Be especially aware of the spacing between the swimmers throughout the routine.

The next section will present some factors to consider when choreographing a team. Remember that the choreography is limited only by the creativity of the coach and the swimmers. Also keep in mind the other elements of choreography that have been previously mentioned, such as synchronization, fluidity, and creative action.

Team Choreography

The team event ranks as the highlight of synchronized swimming, providing a spectacular demonstration of the true meaning of synchronization. Choreographing an interesting five-minute program of athletic strength and showmanship for four to eight individuals presents quite a challenge.

The first aspect to consider when writing a team routine is the skill level of the swimmers. Include only those strokes, figures, positions, actions, and pool patterns that reflect their ability. Making a list as shown below can help you keep in mind difficulty, variety, fluidity, and the strongest qualities of the swimmers.

Even the most advanced swimmers find that basic positions are easier to match, execute similarly, synchronize, and put to music.

The use of the pool and pool patterns are other components to consider in choreo-

Strokes	Positions	Actions
Front Crawl	Vertical	Twists
Back Crawl	Heron	Spins (180°, 360°, Open)
Sidestroke	Crane	Rotations
Breast Stroke	Knight	Jump Outs
Butterfly	Ballet Leg	Rockets
Eggbeater:	Front/Back Pike	Lifts
Single Arm	Front/Back Tuck	Floats
Double Arm	Split	Roll Outs
		Walkouts

graphing the team event. A routine should include a variety of simple to difficult patterns—scattered, single line, open (circle, square, diamond), and diagonal. The transitions from one to the next should be fluid and easily recognized. When placing swimmers in the pattern, put the strongest toward the center and weaker swimmers at the outside. The routine should cover the whole pool, moving side to side as well as up and down. The patterns should change as frequently as the swimmers are capable of making a smooth change without losing their positions. Charting out the patterns before trying them in the water usually helps alleviate any confusion.

Creative action can contribute greatly to team choreography because so much can be done with four to eight swimmers. Consider using the following actions: a float, a partner action, a group action, a peel-off (individuals break off from a pattern one at a time), a Ballet Leg line, and a four-plus-four (four swimmers are executing one action while four others are doing something else). Exercise as much creativity as possible in choreographing the deckwork and the ending. The beginning should capture the audience's interest and the ending must be memorable. Wherever you include creative action, however, it will add highlights and fun. There is nothing quite like the spirit achieved from working together to create a team for the coach and swimmers involved.

The strength, flexibility, and endurance so vital to executing good synchronized swimming routines can only be attained and maintained through proper conditioning. Chapter 7 presents sections on Swimming and Sculling Conditioning and on Flexibility.

Chapter 7: Conditioning

Like any athlete, the synchronized swimmer must be in good condition in order to perform at his or her optimal level. Improvement in the swimmer's fitness level will be reflected in the quality of the performance. Because a synchronized swimming routine lasts 3½ to 5 minutes, the synchronized swimmer needs the same cardiorespiratory endurance as a middle-distance swimmer. There are many training regimens used by coaches for middle-distance swimmers. This chapter includes a sample workout for a middle-distance swimmer that can be adapted to synchronized swimming.

Synchronized swimmers have a unique need for strength in sculling. Repetitive sculling offers one kind of effective training, but coaches can make these exercises more enjoyable for the swimmers by using the sculling workout on pp. 100-103.

Flexibility training should be incorporated into the synchronized swim program. A flexible swimmer can execute better movements and transitions, which in turn enhance the fluidity of the movement. Recommended procedures for stretching and stretching exercises, also presented in this chapter, can help swimmers become more flexible.

Sample Middle-Distance Workout

The synchronized swimmer can be compared to a middle-distance swimmer because both expend energy for approximately 3½ to 5 minutes. In addition to using the sample workout presented here, the synchro coach can seek guidance and direction from the competitive swim coach of the local swim club, high school, or collegiate swim team.

For more information on swimming training, see *The Science of Swimming* by James E. Counsilman and *Swimming Faster* by Ernest W. Maglischo.

The following sample yardages of middle-distance workouts can be used by synchronized swimmers.

Age	Daily Yardage	Weekly Total
10 and under	600-1,200	2,400-4,800
11 to 12	1,000-2,000	5,000-10,000
13 to 14	2,000-4,000	10,000-20,000
Seniors	4,000-6,000	40,000

To make the workouts interesting, the synchro coach can employ various forms of training to cover the recommended number of yards. The most common is interval training. As the name implies, interval training is a series of repeated bouts of swimming alternated with periods of relief. Four factors should be considered in interval training: The number of swims, the distance of each swim, the speed of the swims, and the amount of rest between each swim. An example of a training series can be written as:

12	×	200 yards	/	60 seconds	–	2:30
number of swims	times	distance of swims	on	rest between swims	at	average speed

This same series is most commonly written 12 × 200/3:30 – 2:30 freestyle. The 3:30 is the send-off time. The 200-yard freestyle should be completed in about 2 minutes and 30 seconds. Every 3 minutes 30 seconds, the swimmers are sent off for another repeat. If the interval requires more than three or four swims, lengthen the rest period between sets. This will allow the swimmer to recover sufficiently to execute the remaining swims showing a reasonable amount of quality. Using the same example, 12 × 200/3:30 – 2:30, a rest interval (R.I.) of 2 to 3 minutes should be included after every 3rd or 4th swim:

3 sets of 4 × 200/3:30 – 2:30, 3:00 R.I.

The coach and swimmers can create as many different intervals as they want. Varying the yardage between 25 to 500 yards will help make the workouts interesting. The following guideline for the rest intervals from *Swimming Faster* will help the swimmer to maintain 80 to 90% of her maximum speed on the intervals.

25 yards	5 seconds rest
50 yards	10 seconds rest
100 yards	30 seconds rest
200 yards	60 seconds rest

A form of interval training called broken swimming can also give the workout some variety. A particular distance is broken into parts and repeated in sequence with a minimal rest period between the parts. The total time, minus the rest periods, is compared with the best time for that distance for each swimmer. To monitor the quality of the broken swims, the coach should keep a chart of or post each swimmer's best times. An example of a 400-yard freestyle broken swim might be:

2 × 50/40 – 35
2 × 100/1:30 – 1:20
2 × 50/40 – 35

Here again, the coach and/or swimmers can be creative. Two forms of training that will add variety to the swimming workout are marathon training, a long swim at a constant pace, and fartlek training, which is varied according to the coach's and/or swimmer's specifications. Any combination of speed (moderate to fast) or strokes and any variety of swimming, pulling, and kicking can be used over a long, continuous distance.

Finally, hypoxic training can and should be used in the synchronized swimmer's workout. This form of training reduces the breathing rate to reduce the oxygen supply, thus enhancing both the aerobic and anaerobic training effects. According to Maglischo in *Swimming Faster*, hypoxic training has no known training effect except an improved ability to hold the breath. An average synchronized swimmer spends between 30 to 50% of the routine underwater for periods of approximately 5 to 30 seconds. The more advanced swimmers stay under for up to 50 seconds while executing a series of hybrids and transitions. Although swimmers are not necessarily encouraged or required to spend

a long period of time underwater, those who do can develop better breath control through hypoxic training. To illustrate hypoxic training, refer back to the interval training example; 3 sets of 4 × 200/3:30 - 2:30, 3:00 R.I., freestyle. Each 200-yard swim could include the following breathing pattern:

1st length, breath every 3rd stroke
2nd length, breath every 5th stroke
3rd length, breath every 7th stroke
4th length, breath every 9th stroke
5th length, breath every 9th stroke
6th length, breath every 7th stroke
7th length, breath every 5th stroke
8th length, breath every 3rd stroke

This can be reversed so that the breath is every ninth stroke on the first and eighth lengths and every third stroke on the fourth and fifth lengths. Again, there is room for creativity, though this training method is used primarily for freestyle and to some extent for the butterfly.

In order to write an appropriate workout, the coach must know the condition of the swimmers. Knowing how fast they can swim a 25-, 50-, 100-, 200-, 400- and/or 500-yard freestyle will help the coach develop an effective workout. Through a minimal amount of trial and error, the coach can administer a good workout and have the swimmers finish their prescribed yardage at the same time. Using available local resources will help you develop quality middle-distance workouts. The following sample middle-distance workout was adapted from *The Science of Swimming* (Counsilman, 1968), using interval and hypoxic training for the senior-level swimmer. Reducing the yardage and increasing the swim times and rest intervals will adapt the workout for younger, less experienced swimmers.

1. Warm-up 500-yard freestyle, beginning at 50% speed and increasing to 75% speed.

2. Kick 200-yard flutter kick, hard.

3. Pull 200-yard freestyle, hard, 3:00 R.I.

4. Swim 4 × 400/10:00 − 6:00, hypoxic.

5. Swim 200-yard backstroke, easy (50% speed).

6. Kick 3 × 300/8:00 − 6:00, flutter.

7. Pull 6 × 150/3:00 − 2:15, freestyle, hypoxic.

8. Swim 200-yard backstroke, easy (50% speed).

Total distance: 4,700 yards.

The next section introduces the concept of building strength through the use of sculling conditioning. A sample workout is offered for use in a 30-minute sculling conditioning regimen.

Sculling Strength

The techniques of sculling were described fully in *Coaching Synchronized Swimming Effectively*. In addition to learning the prescribed movements of the sculls, swimmers must also develop strength in their sculling in order to learn the figures of synchronized swimming. For this reason, training in synchronized swimming must include conditioning for sculling as well as for strokes and kicks.

Most coaches have their swimmers swim lap after lap of each of the standard sculls to develop sculling strength. But swimming lap after lap can get boring. This section introduces some creative ways to incorporate sculls and partial figures to increase strength and flexibility, and as an added benefit, to increase fluidity in the transitional movements. The sculls listed here and the sample 30-minute workout are only suggestions to get you started. Use your imagination to come up with other creative sculling methods.

Sample 30-Minute Sculling Workout

This workout includes three sets of 6 × 25's of sculling, followed by 4 lengths of kicking and then a stationary sculling drill. The kicking lengths are not the only kicking that is done in a workout. They are given here only to relax the arms slightly so that the rest of the workout can be followed. Continuous sculling for 30 minutes would probably cause cramping in the arms, wrists, and hands.

1st set
    2 lengths—left hinge Ballet Legs, head-first and foot-first
    2 lengths—Jumpovers and Backovers
    2 lengths—Ballet Leg stretches, right leg

and left leg
4 lengths—kicking

2nd set
    2 lengths—right hinge Ballet Legs, head-first and foot-first
    2 lengths—Front Walkovers, Back Walkovers
    2 lengths—Swordfish series
    4 lengths—kicking

3rd set
    2 lengths—Flamingo sculls, head-first and foot-first
    1 length—waves
    1 length—double tucks

1 length—front series (Pike, Porpoise, Jumpover)
1 length—back series (Doubles, Barracuda, Dolphin)
4 lengths—kicking

The following provides a detailed description of each of the 30 lengths and the stationary sculling drills.

1st set
Hinge Ballet Legs
Use four sculls in each position. Layout (4), to Bent Knee (4), to Ballet Leg (4), lower leg to a position horizontal to the water (4), raise to Ballet Leg (4), and keep repeating until the end of the length. The leg does not move down to Bent Knee and Layout until the end of the two lengths. The first length is head-first, the second length is foot-first. The left leg is used in this first set.

Jumpovers
Alligator scull (4), to Front Pike Pull Down (4), Jumpover to Back Layout position and Torpedo scull (8), Torpedo scull into a one-half Back Tuck to come up on the stomach and repeat. Do the entire length of Jumpovers.

Backovers
Standard scull (4), Tub position (4), roll over into a half Back Tuck Somersault extending the legs into a Front Layout position, Lobster scull (4), and bend the knees up under the stomach and roll onto the back. Repeat from the beginning until the length is completed.

Ballet Leg Stretches
Standard scull (4), Bent Knee scull (4), Ballet Leg scull (4). Continue Standard scull, moving the leg over the face and trying to keep the head up (touch the knee to the nose) until the leg reaches the surface of the water as the head drops under. When the head is under the hips, rotate the hips (Squid Turn),

and Walkout. Tub turn to begin again. Start with the left leg on the first length and the right leg on the second length.

Kicking
Two lengths each of back flutter kick and side flutter kick.

2nd set
Hinge Ballet Legs
Same as above using the right Ballet Leg.

Front Walkovers
Alligator scull (4), to Front Pike Pull Down (4), first leg over (8), second leg over (8), float up to a half Tub turn, and begin again.

Back Walkovers
Four Reverse Torpedo sculls (4), first leg over (8), second leg over (8), Lobster scull (8), and bring the knees through as in the Backover above. Repeat for the entire length.

Swordfish Series
Canoe scull (4), Swordfish, then Torpedo scull (4), half Tub, rollover to Front Layout position, Canoe scull (4), and Swordasub to point at which the leg normally starts extending. Instead, open leg to Split position and Walkout, half Tub, rollover to Front Layout position, to Canoe (4), Swordasub. When the head surfaces in the Ballet Leg position, continue a foot-first Ballet Leg to the end of the length. Repeat the length.

Kicking
Two lengths each of front flutter and side flutter kick.

3rd set
Flamingo Sculls
One length switches, followed by one length of foot-first changes.

Flamingo Switches
Standard scull (4), Bent Knee position (4), Ballet Leg (4), Flamingo (4), switch

to opposite Flamingo (8), switch again (8), and keep switching for the entire length without returning to the Back Layout.

Flamingo Changes

(Can be done either head-first or foot-first. Because the above length was done head-first, try this one done foot-first.)

Standard scull (4), Bent Knee (4), Ballet Leg (4), Flamingo (4), Doubles (4), first leg down to Flamingo (4), extend first leg into the Back Layout position (4), second leg down to Bent Knee (4), extend the second leg to the Back Layout (4). Repeat the series until the music ends using alternate legs to begin the first bend.

Waves

Torpedo (4), Torpedo scull arching the back until the legs are pointing straight toward the bottom of the pool (4), bring the arms toward the knees as the hips are piked and pull the arms through and overhead as the body is straightened in order to return to the surface in Torpedo scull. Continue to the end of the length.

Double-Tucks

Standard scull (4), Tub position (4), Double Ballet Legs (8), bend the knees down into the eyes and tuck, extend to Front Layout, and begin again.

Front Series

Alligator scull (4), Front Pike Pull Down (4), to Front Pike Somersault. Alligator (4), to Front Pike Pull Down (4), to Porpoise. Alligator (4), to Front Pike Pull Down (4), to Jumpover. Torpedo to the end of the length.

Back Series

Standard scull (4), Tub position (4), Double Ballet Legs (4), submerged Doubles (4), Barracuda (4), control the descent of the Barracuda, and surface as a Dolphin.

Kicking

Two lengths of rotating flutter kick. Side kicking (8), front flutter (8), side flutter (8), back flutter (8).

Two lengths of Eggbeater walks, one forward and one backward.

Stationary Sculling Drills

The following drills should be done in place with no traveling. These drills will help increase strength and will be helpful in figure competition that requires stationary execution. The first four exercises are another method for developing breath control. The slower the execution, the longer the swimmer must hold her breath. All of the drills can be enhanced by music, if desired. Be sure to tell the swimmers the counts for each of the figure actions. These drills enable the swimmers to work simultaneously on synchronization, breath control, development of sculling strength, and controlled execution of the figure action.

Joins-Porpoise to Crane position, scull (8), join other leg, scull (8), then descend. Do this four to eight times.

Catalinas Up and Down-Ballet Leg position, Catalina Rotation to Crane position, scull (8), reverse the rotation (Reverse Catalina) to come up, scull in Ballet Leg position (8).

Continue to rotate down and up, keeping the Ballet Leg up for four to eight rotations down and up.

Crane Tips-This is a more advanced skill that is not covered in this book. You might give it a try anyway. Ballet Leg position, tip back as in a Crane start, Crane position, scull (8), tip back up as in a Reverse Crane, scull (8), and keep tipping from the Ballet Leg to the Crane and back up four to eight times.

Musical Ballet Legs-Select a favorite piece of current pop music and have the swimmers do Ballet Legs for the entire record. These can be done on counts of fours, eights, Flamingo switches and changes, round Ballet

Legs, multiple extensions, side tips, hinge legs, and so forth. Do not let them put their legs down until the end of the music.

Note: This sample workout gives you an idea of how to help the swimmers improve their skills. As these skills become more developed, you can increase the number of sculls in each position from two to four to eight and so on.

In addition to impoving the cardiorespiratory endurance and sculling strength, a strong swimmer also needs to increase her flexibility. Flexibility enhances the fluid component of the synchronized swimming routine.

Flexibility Exercises

Developing flexibility is a key objective in a synchronized swimmer's program. A flexible swimmer is more fluid and versatile and can execute a greater range of motion and variety of movement. Flexibility is also essential for the proper performance of many figures, especially those that require Splits, Walkouts, and Back Pikes.

Flexibility can be developed in phases. The first phase involves warming all the muscle groups. Cold muscles are relatively inelastic. If a swimmer tries to stretch her muscles while cold, she may stretch or tear her tendons instead and end up with weak, injury prone joints. Swimmers can warm their muscles easily by walking in place or around the room to music, and then doing a three- to four-minute series of arm circles and some upper body exercises.

Preparatory stretching is done in the second phase. These stretches gradually lengthen and relax the muscle groups to prepare for the deeper stretches in the third phase. Breathing and relaxation are crucial factors

in both stretching phases. An awareness of their breathing patterns will help the swimmers relax. A breath should be long and continuous and feel as if it is circulating throughout the entire body. The cycle of breath should match the timing of the stretches—that is, with each exhalation, the muscles should release tension and relax.

All stretches should be performed slowly and gently, increased slightly with each exhalation, and sustained for at least 30 seconds. The swimmers should not jerk or bounce while stretching because a protective reflex will only cause the muscle to contract, which can cause tearing. Whenever possible, gravity and body weight (rather than pulling) should be used to gradually stretch farther. Make sure the swimmers *never* continue a stretch to the point of pain or discomfort.

Becoming flexible takes time and patience. Flexibility sessions should be held 3 times a week for 30 minutes. Within five weeks, improvements in flexibility should be noted.

Stretches

Neck Stretches

Begin with the neck straight and stretch tall. Keep the face and jaw relaxed throughout the exercise.

Starting Position-Place one hand on top of the head with the fingers to the back. Move the chin toward the neck as the head is lowered to the chest. Do not let the chin touch the chest. (1A)

Stretch Forward-Gently pull the head forward and down. In this forward position, move the head side to side as if saying no and hold each tipped position for 30 seconds. Return to the starting position. (1B)

Stretch Sideways-Place the left hand on top of the head with the fingers pointing to the right ear. Bend the head to the side so the left ear is over the left shoulder. Make sure the face stays forward, not up or down. Gently pull the head toward the shoulder. Keep the shoulders down and relaxed. Hold for 30 seconds keeping the face, jaw, and mouth relaxed. Return to the starting position. (1C-1D)

Stretch to the other side. Return to the starting position. (1E-1F)

Diagonal Stretching-Return to the starting position shown in 1A. Pull the head down diagonally to the right and then to the left. This stretches the part of the neck that was not stretched in the previous exercises. (1G)

Shoulder Stretches

Underneath Stretch-Clasp hands behind the hips and lift them behind the back; bending forward will allow gravity to help the stretch. This may also be done standing. (2A)

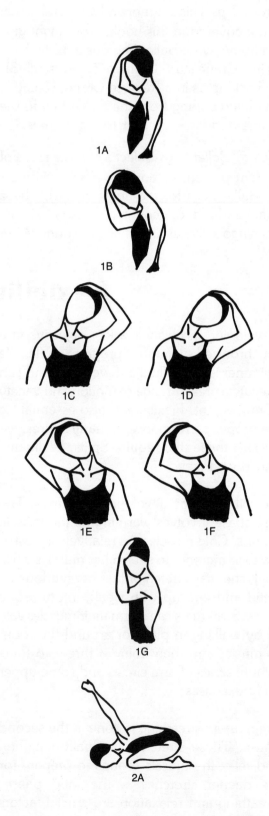

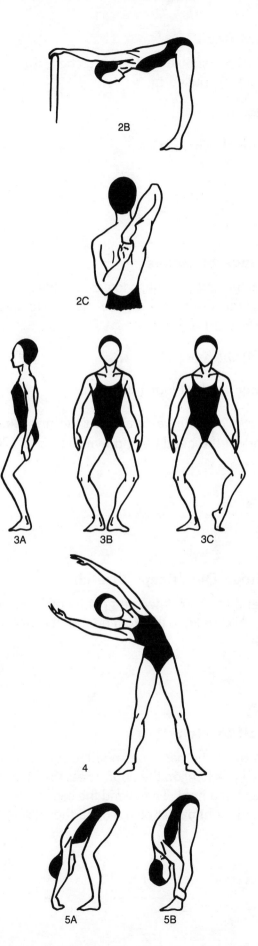

Overhead Stretch-Hold a bar or the back of a chair and gently press the shoulders down. (2B)

Under/Over Stretch-Grasp the fingers behind the shoulders, using a small towel if the fingers will not reach. (2C)

Pliés

Slowly bend and straighten knees to warm up the ankles and legs. Keep the knees pointed directly over the toes. *Never* turn the toes out farther than the knees.

Parallel (3A)

Turned Out (3B)

With High Arch in the Foot (3C)

Side Stretch

Stretch from the waist up only; keep the hips even with equal weight on both feet. (4)

Hamstring Stretch

Plié (Bent Knees)-Hang over and relax. (5A)

Straighten Knees-Grab the ankles and gently pull as the knees straighten. Never lock the knees fully. (5B)

Flat Back

The back should be flat, not arched. Keep the stomach pulled in.

Plié (6A)

Straight Knees (6B)

Lunge Stretches

Let the hipbones hang toward the floor, keeping the front heel on the ground to avoid straining the knee.

Straight Knee (7A)

Knee to the Floor (7B)

Backward Lunge-Straighten the front knee and let the head hang down toward it. (7C)

Lunge Quadriceps Stretch

Bend the back knee and gently pull the foot in. Always keep the front heel on the ground. (8)

Calf Stretch

Keeping the back toes pointed forward and the back heel on the floor, press the hips forward and hold. Then bend the back knee forward slightly to stretch a bit farther. (9A-9B)

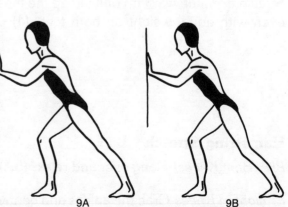

Back Curves (Contractions)

From a straight back position, keep the shoulders in line with the hips and curve the spine backward. The belly should feel like it is being scooped out. Avoid slumping the shoulders. This exercise may be done seated or standing. (10A-10B).

Gluteal Stretch

Gently pull the knee to the chest and hold. (11)

Spine Twist

Hold the knee with the opposite hand and let it hang across the body; keeping the legs and feet relaxed. (12A).

Gently roll back over to same side. Arm extended in the air. (12B)

Back Stretch (Cobra)

Press up from the floor on the hands, keeping the shoulders down and away from the neck. Always curl the back after the arched stretches to release the lower back. (13A-13B)

Frog Stretch

Press the knees gently down towards the floor. (14)

Leg Stretch on the Back

Pull one leg gently toward the face, keeping one hand behind the knee to avoid overstretching the tendons. (15)

Straddles

Reach out and hang to the center, to the right, and to the left. Keep the knees facing the ceiling; do not let them roll forward.

Center (16A)

Right (16B)

Left (16C)

Splits

Warm up with lunge stretches. Slide the front foot out from the backward lunge, until a stretch is felt and hold the position. (17)

Oversplits

Back Knee Bent-Bend the back knee and pull the foot in. (18A)

Front Foot Lifted-Place the front foot on a slightly higher surface than the floor and slide into a split. Dictionaries provide a good elevated surface for this exercise. (18B)

Partner Resistance Stretches

These stretches are based on a reflex that signals a strongly contracted (working) muscle to relax. A partner brings the swimmer to a stretched position. The swimmer then contracts the muscle group for five to ten seconds, pushing against her partner's pressure. Her partner can then help her stretch farther because the reflex has decreased the muscles' natural resistance to the stretch. Both partners must be very careful and communicate well when doing these stretches to avoid stretching past the point of pain and possibly causing an injury.

Leg Stretch on the Back-This is basically the same stretch as Number 15, with the aid of a partner. Partner A tries to push her leg away from her face against partner B's pressure. Partner B then gently pushes the leg back toward partner A's face as partner A relaxes. (19A)

Leg Stretch on the Side-Follow the instructions for Number 19, but do it on the side, stretching the leg toward the shoulder. (If the swimmer is very flexible, the leg can be stretched to slightly behind the shoulder.) (19B)

Hip Joint Stretch on the Stomach-Partner B pulls partner A's knee up with one hand, holding the corresponding side of the hip down with the other. Partner A tries to push her knee back to the floor against partner B's pressure. Partner B can then pull the knee higher as partner A relaxes. (19C)

Shoulder Stretch-Partner A holds her arms out to the sides with palms forward, and partner B pulls them directly back until a stretch is felt. Partner A then tries to pull her hands forward again as partner B holds them in place. When partner A relaxes, partner B can gently pull partner A's hands farther back. Partner A should keep her stomach pulled in to avoid arching her back. (19D)

Chapter 8 will discuss ways to implement conditioning and practice programs that correspond to the space available, the coach's time, numbers of swimmers and coaches, and other logistical factors. The chapter also discusses overall year-round program planning, the factors to consider for an age group program, and considerations for traveling with the team for the first time.

Chapter 8: Organizing the Team

This chapter offers guidelines on starting a club team that you can follow or modify to suit your particular needs at your pool or club. If you need advice on organizational decisions, talk to other synchronized swimming coaches and teachers in your local area. You can also obtain more information from the national office: Synchro-USA, 901 West New York Street, Indianapolis, Indiana 46223, (317) 633-2000.

The first part of this chapter discusses ways to organize your practices in order to make the most of your pool time. The next section deals with age group programs, and the last section covers planning for the first trip with your team. (This information is worth reviewing even if you have already undertaken this feat.)

Program Planning

The primary consideration of any synchronized swimming program must be the de-

velopment of swimming skills. Swimmers must first have a good knowledge of the strokes, and stroke development and conditioning should continue throughout all phases of training.

To develop a yearly plan, first divide the year into its seasonal blocks: the fall conditioning phase, the early competitive season, the active competitive season and the post-season phase. Each phase requires a different plan.

Planning the program demands far more than determining the content of the workouts. You must also consider physical factors such as the time and space allocated, the number of swimmers to be included, and the number of coaches available to help. Although a work-out for 40 athletes conducted by a single coach will look vastly different from a work-out for 40 with four or more coaches, both include the same basic program elements.

In addition, plans must be made for any off-site training such as weight training or aerobic, dance, and gymnastic classes geared to synchro, as well as land drills done off site or at the pool. You also need to coordinate efforts with the parents group in taking care of many outside activities, such as hosting competitions, making arrangements for travel and housing, raising funds, obtaining costumes, and handling communications.

Time

The length of time available for the workout must be considered in the planning. Whenever possible, younger swimmers and older swimmers should work out at separate times as should more experienced swimmers and novices. In planning the program, keep in mind that the younger swimmers have shorter attention spans than older swimmers do and therefore should have a shorter period of figure training. Older swimmers both want and need the additional figure time. When both age groups are in the pool at the same time, it is difficult to vary the length of time allocated to each.

In general, senior and older age group swimmers should have at least a two-hour workout. One and one-half hours works well for the younger age group swimmers, and novices should have only a one-hour workout.

Try to schedule the longest time periods possible because you will always find a way to use the time advantageously. If you request only a short period when the group is young and new, you may find yourself frozen into a time spot that will not allow for the development of more experienced swimmers. Take as much time as you can get, and then try to find the way to fill it and finance it.

Space

Consider the pool size in determining the number of swimmers for each workout. The following guidelines will help you determine where they will actually practice the various skills.

- Swimming training is best done with one swimmer per lane, but you can put up to ten in each lane using a circle pattern.
- Scull training can be done in a single lane

using circle patterning. It is better, however, to have two lanes so that you have one place for propulsive and another for supportive scull development.

- Figure training can be done at the end or side of the pool in deep water. You can fit 4 or 5 swimmers working with partners across the deep end of the standard 25-yard pool.

- Routines should be done in a pool that is at least 25 yards long and should take up all the space out to the edges. This means swim or scull training cannot go on during routine practice, but some figures can fit around the edges.

In general, the bigger the pool, the easier it

is to fit in all the training areas during the same time period (see Figure 8.1-8.3). Of the pools for swimmers—the 60-foot pool, the standard 25-yard pool (42 by 75 feet), the standard Olympic pool, the 25-yard by 25-meter, and the standard water polo pool (25 by 33 meters), the favorite is the 25 yards by 25 meters. This size offers the best space for developing all areas of skills during a single workout.

In considering space, also think of whether you have to share a pool with swim classes or other groups, such as divers, speed swimmers, or lap swimmers. These considerations will determine where you place the various synchro groups for their skill development.

Number of Instructors

In general, the ratio of a teacher for every 8 to 10 swimmers is ideal. The only better situation would be to have additional figure coaches available for that part of the workout. Whether you can achieve this ratio (1:10) depends on the number in the group and whether or not you have been able to secure extra coaching help. You should take personal responsibility for the development of no more than two team routines in a season.

Finding help can be a problem. Consider, of course, former synchro and speed swimmers. Others who can be trained to cover certain areas of the workout are physical education teachers, Red Cross instructors, and recreation department teachers. At first, you may find yourself spending a great deal of time teaching the teachers. In the long run, however, they can be of great assistance to you.

Music Time

Allowing enough music time for all the routines you plan to do is one of the most critical aspects of synchronized swimming planning. Even with careful planning, it seems there is never enough.

Accenting the team and group routines is of prime importance for maximum development of a group. It is also the aspect that most groups like best. Team spirit and helpfulness

are developed when team routines are accented with solos, duets, and trios given to those who have attained a certain skill level.

The following plan was used during the 1970s and 1980s with a group of 90 swimmers who had a maximum of 4 hours of pool time, Monday through Friday, and 5 hours on Saturday. Four to five coaches were on deck.

Sample Schedule for Music Time

Monday-Wednesday	5-6:30 p.m.	Novice and beginner class teams and trios
	7-9:00 p.m.	Senior teams and trios
Tuesday-Thursday	5-6:30 p.m.	12 and under teams and trios
	7-9:00 p.m.	13 and over teams and trios
Friday	5-6:30 p.m.	12 and under solos and duets
	7-9:00 p.m.	13 and over solos and duets
Saturday	7-10:00 a.m.	Senior teams and duets, 13 and over teams and duets
	10:00 a.m.-12 Noon	12 and under teams and duets, novice teams
Note:	6:30-7 p.m. daily	Optional time for solo and duet work on a prescheduled basis. Also optional figure-work time because only the music coach has a group. The other three to four coaches can either help the younger swimmers staying in or older swimmers who come early.

Also note that this schedule was for music only. Swimmers also work out and have extra figure work on days when they do not have music time.

Content

In planning the workout, include all elements of the sport to ensure proper development of the athletes. Some coaches accent certain elements more in one season than another. For example, they work more on strokes in the fall and on figure work during the competitive season. In general, however, all workouts should cover the four basic areas of synchro training:

- Swimming skills, all standard strokes as well as kicking and Eggbeater.

- Sculling skills, both propulsive and supportive.

- Figure skills, both compulsories and routine figures, parts and whole.

- Music skills, both training drills and competitive routines.

Dividing the workout into a warm-up period followed by four rotations, one for each of the program areas (swim, scull, figures, music) works well for most of the season. For example, you might schedule a 10- to 15-minute warm-up period, followed by four 25-minute rotations for the four program areas. Following such a schedule ensures that no area is neglected, as often happens when a coach becomes overly engrossed in a specific routine or figure.

Logistics

The following samples show how and where to set up workouts for a varying number of coaches and different pool sizes. These are only general guidelines; you will have to find the arrangement that works best for you. These examples are worth considering, however, because they have made maximum use of the allocated time and space.

20 swimmers, 1 coach, 2 hours 42 ft by 75 ft pool

10-minute warm-up, 2-3 per lane

25-minute swim workout, 2-3 per lane

25-minute sculling workout, wave formation

10-minute figure instruction by coach

40 minutes. Figure practice by pairs while coach watches routines

20 swimmers, 2 coaches, 2 hours 42 ft by 75 ft pool

(See Figure 8.1)

10-minute warm-up, 2-3 per lane

50 minutes. One coach works with half of the group on swimming while another coach works with the other half on sculling. Change groups for the second 25 minutes.

50 minutes. One coach watches routines while the other coaches the figures; switch after 25 minutes.

40 swimmers, 1 coach, 2 hours 42 ft by 75 ft pool

10-minute warm-up, 6 per lane, circle pattern

25-minute swim workout

25-minute sculling workout

10-minute figure instruction

40-minutes. Coach watches routines while swimmers pair up for figure work.

40 swimmers, 2 coaches, 2 hours 42 ft by 75 ft pool

(See Figure 8.2)

10-minute warm-up, 4 per lane, circle pattern

50 minutes. One coach takes half of the group for 25 minutes of swimming, while the other takes other half for 25 minutes of sculling. Change groups for second 25 minutes.

50 minutes. One coach watches routines while the other coaches figures.

40 swimmers, 4 coaches, 2 hours 25 yd by 25 m pool

(See Figure 8.2)

10-minute warm-up, 8 per lane, circle pattern

Four 25-minute rotations of swimming, sculling, figures, routines, 10 in each group. The advantage of four rotations is that different groups start with different skills on different days and can make use of the coaches' special talents.

80 swimmers, 5-7 coaches, 2 hours 25 yd by 25 m pool

(See Figure 8.2)

10-minute warm-up, 8 per lane, circle pattern

Four 25-minute-rotations of swimming (1 coach), sculling (1-2 coaches), figures (2-3 coaches), routines (1 coach), 20 in each group.

40 swimmers, 4-5 coaches, 2 hours 50 m Olympic pool

(See Figure 8.3)

10-minute warm-up across width

Four 25-minute rotations of swimming (1

coach), sculling (1 coach), figures (2 coaches), routines (1 coach), 10 in each group.

80 swimmers, 5-7 coaches, 2 hours 50 m Olympic pool

(See Figure 8.3)
10-minute warm-up across width

Four 25-minute rotations of swimming (1 coach), sculling (1-2 coaches), figures (2-3 coaches), routines (1 coach), 20 in each group.

Now that the logistics are reasonably taken care of, everyone has to look at their own situation and figure out the best use of time and space allocated.

Figure 8.1 Workout pattern for 20 swimmers and 2 coaches.

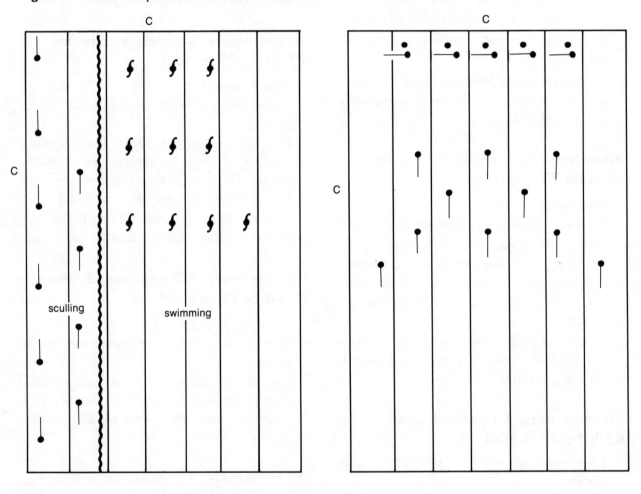

Figure 8.2 Sample workout patterns for 40 swimmers.

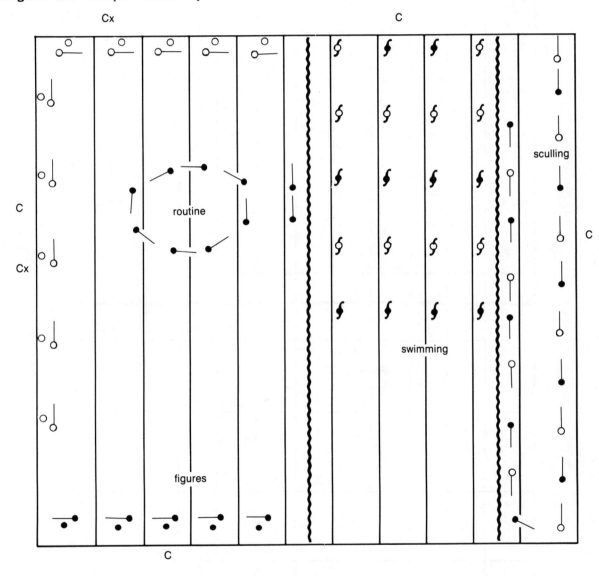

C = Coach
♀♀ = Swimmers
Cx = Extra Coach

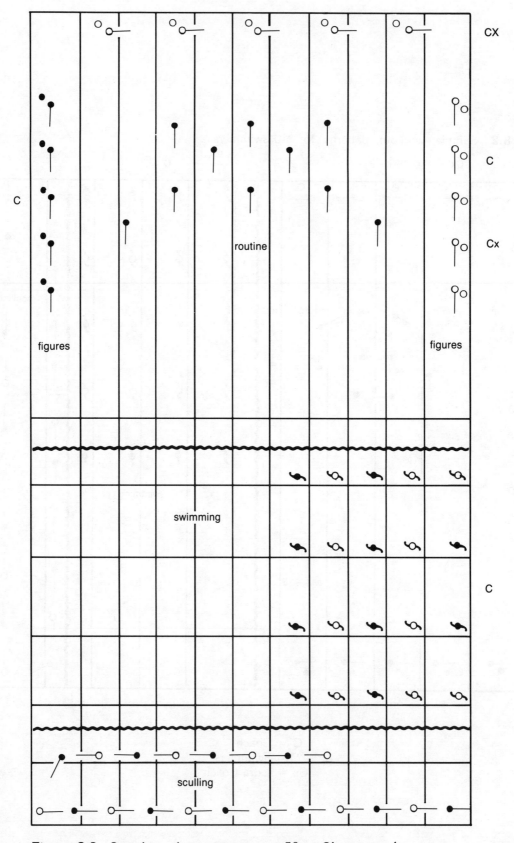

Figure 8.3 Sample workout patterns in a 50 m Olympic pool.

Training Principles

The following basic principles should also be considered in workout planning.

Progression

The intensity of the workout must be increased in logical progression. Workouts right after the summer vacation must be easier than those done after the swimmers have become conditioned. As the swimmers become increasingly fit, the workouts should become increasingly difficult.

Overload

The exercises must be stressful enough to produce a physical change in the athlete's body. Only by overload can the exercise be beneficial in terms of improving muscle strength, flexibility, and coordination.

Adaptability

Workouts must be flexible and make allowances for individual differences such as age, growth, development, and skill level.

Specificity

The training must meet the specific needs of synchronized swimming performance. For example, playing tennis on three of the workout days would probably not enhance the synchronized swimming performance. However, synchronized swimmers might benefit from such activities as aerobic dance and gymnastics on three days without pool time.

Monitoring

Athletes need to be evaluated periodically to determine the effectiveness of the training. Keep records of such factors as flexibility measurements, time trials, heart rate checks, and weight. Athletes must understand the importance of monitoring their own improvements.

Goal Setting

Athletes and coaches should set a series of short-term, realistic goals in order to achieve the long-term goals. The goals should include both those of the individual and those of the group.

The Yearly Plan

The training year is typically divided into four phases: conditioning, early competitive, competitive, and postcompetitive. The following guidelines can be used for swimmers of all levels.

Conditioning Phase (generally September through December in the U.S.)

The emphasis during this phase, for all levels of swimmers, should be on selfimprovement. Stress quality workouts, stroking, and kicking laps, so that the swimmers will build endurance and strength and develop good basic techniques in all strokes, sculls, and figures.

Beginners should swim 1,000 to 2,000 yards a day, depending on their ability. Work on technique development in all strokes and sculls, having them swim mostly 25-yard repeats with corrections at the end of the length. Do some endurance training with 100- and 200-yard repeats.

Intermediate and advanced swimmers should swim 2,000 to 6,000 yards a day. Focus on endurance swims of 200 to 1,500 yards while continuing some stroke corrections.

All groups should thoroughly review (or learn) all the sculls and basic body positions, as well as all techniques for beginners and intermediate figures. Flexibility, grace, and coordination should be developed during pool and land practice.

The coach should be choosing and editing music, developing ideas for choreography, and observing the swimmers in order to select solo, duet, trio, and team members by the end of the conditioning phase.

Early Competitive (generally January through March in the U.S.)

Goals should be reviewed and adjusted if necessary. The emphasis during this phase is on overall development of the figures and routines. Quality work is increasingly demanded.

Strength and endurance development tapers to a maintainance level; swimming laps decrease as specific synchro laps increase.

Beginners taper from 2,000 to 1,200 yards. As the routines are developed, swimming laps are replaced by sprints for lung capacity, strength maintenance, and warm-up purposes. Endurance is developed and maintained during routine swimming, if the group has sufficient time. Even with limited pool time, however, some conditioning swimming must be continued.

Intermediate and advanced workouts taper from 6,000 to 2,000 yards. The other changes are similar to those made for beginners.

Choreography is completed during this phase, beginning with the routines for the earliest scheduled competition. Quality is stressed in figure and routine swimming.

Competitive (generally April through July/August in U.S.)

Practice schedules remain the same as in the early competitive phase with the emphasis shifting to efficiency in routines and perfection in figures. Always demand quality.

Conditioning is at the maintenance level, taking one-fourth of the total pool time. All groups swim about 1,000 yards each workout with many routine repeats.

Quality is demanded constantly in every detail. (The video tape can play a major role now because it allows the swimmers to see every minute correction.) Every figure should be practiced as if it were being performed in competition at that very moment. Demand that the swimmers make an intense, concentrated effort on every figure.

Postcompetitive (generally July/August in the U.S.)

Stress fun through diversions in normal workout activities. Play water polo and pool games, or funny relays or stage a watershow. Vary the workouts so they are different from those of the other phases, but reserve some time for upgrading overall strength, endurance, and techniques.

The coach should help the swimmer to recognize weak areas and learn how to overcome them. To do this, the swimmers and the coach should analyze the year's record, and together make plans for the coming season.

Age Group Programs

The primary function of an age group program is developmental. This means the athletes should be learning the basics of the sport, while having fun and preparing for the future. At this level, there should be minimal pressure with maximum fun. The coach should try to give each athlete some measure of personal success in what is probably their first involvement in organized sport. This initial experience will greatly affect the swimmer's self-image as an athlete and as a person. Keeping these basic coaching fundamentals and accomplishment goals in mind, begin thinking about developing a sport-specific program that can be used to reach this end.

During the summer and fall recruiting programs, encourage tryouts from youngsters of similar age and ability. Then when it comes time to begin routines in earnest, there should be enough participants of compatible age groups to formulate team routines with a minimum of age-group crossing.

Prepare an intensive fall training program. Explain to the new athletes the importance of this preparation ground for doing synchronized swimming well. Most youngsters who sign up for a beginning level program will *not* expect to jump right into an intensive lap swimming situation. They will want to know when they will begin to do all the other things they have seen on television or at a watershow.

It helps to explain immediately what synchronized swimming is all about. Using older, more experienced swimmers from your club as an example will make the coaching much easier. Setting up a big/little sister/brother program at this time can also help.

As you begin in earnest, include conditioning on land as well as in the water. Be sure to offer a lot of variety during each practice, while always including the essential basics, such as basic figure positions and sculling. Each workout must include stretching and extension work on land. Include lots of sit-ups and push-ups to develop muscular strength. The swimmers should swim lengths of all four strokes and work on all of the kicks presented in *Coaching Synchronized Swimming Effectively* and drills devised to combine strokes and kicks. In addition, you should introduce all of the sculls and the Eggbeater and Ballet Leg drills immediately. To overcome the new athlete's natural frustration, focus on praise backed up by very consistent instruction techniques.

Introduce music as an integral part of the sport at this time. Not only will it add variety to the daily practice routine, but it will tell you immediately which athletes understand the concept of performing to music. This knowledge will be helpful later in choosing teammates for duets, trios, and teams.

Continue this intensive program for 8 to 10 weeks. Toward the end, introduce parts of the figures that will be needed for the first meet of the year as well as suitable optionals. When selecting optionals, keep in mind the ability of these beginners. Do not rob them of learning the basics by giving them figures that skip over important developmental steps. Focusing on *parts* of figures at this point will help you to assign each swimmer optional figures of appropriate difficulty.

After completing the fall training program, your routine music should be ready to go and the choreography completed. Adjustments and changes can be made as you teach the routine, but the basic patterns, strokes, and figures should all be in place. It is unlikely that the age group swimmer should or could make major routine choreography decisions, though a swimmer who is a natural at choreography occasionally comes along. Your goal in most instances, however, is for the swimmer to perform a comprehensive routine that has been written to her age and ability level. At this beginning level, the difficulty of team routines should match the low to middle abilities of the performers.

Everyone begins with team first. No matter how many swimmers there are in the club, if there are enough for teams, start there first. Try to build a sense of team unity, pride, and function. Don't waste precious time building groups of individuals rather than teammates.

Based on their performance at practice, determine the obvious selections for additional routines (trios, duets, and solos). In most cases, you will be able to decide very quickly. Solo, duet, and trio routines are for those athletes who are making the greatest and most effortless contribution to the team—those who catch on quickly and do not need the music to be stopped over and over to "get something." These extra routines are for those who can and do work well independently, those who can and do help others, and those who can grow on their own without constant tutelage. Performing an extra routine should be an honor that is not given to everyone.

As the competitive season progresses, be flexible and keep the program growing and changing without losing the basic developmental focus. During the fall training season, it is important to establish a sense of commitment among the swimmers' teams that will hold them together through the competitive season. This commitment will help you further develop unity that will contribute greatly to the success of the team and also the club.

Traveling for the First Time

Going away from home to compete can be both an exciting and an anxiety-producing experience for the athlete, the coach, and the parents. The following guidelines are designed to prepare everyone concerned to handle the experience.

First, suggest that your team form a travel committee composed of a parent from each age group and the coach. Give copies of the meet flyer to the committee members as soon as possible. The committee makes hotel, bus, or plane reservations and arranges car pools as needed. Make sure that copies of maps are distributed to the drivers and that the families of the swimmers are given the name, address, and telephone number of the hotel and pool. The meet headquarters is usually the best choice for a hotel and gives the swimmers the opportunity to meet other athletes. When choosing a motel or hotel, consider proximity to the pool and reasonable restaurants. Designate a parent at home to receive phone calls from the coach or chaperone concerning arrival times.

The second step is to call a meeting of the swimmers who will be traveling. Knowing what to expect is very important for the swimmer, and it takes only a few minutes to explain to them what they need to bring along. Make sure you cover suits, warm-ups, tapes, the amount of money they will need, and other pertinent topics (see checklist for swimmers). Coaches, too, should compile a list of important items to pack (see coach's checklist).

Swimmer's Checklist for the Trip

1. Practice suit, competition suits, and headpieces

2. Cap, goggles, noseclips, unflavored gelatin, bobby pins, make-up

3. Sweatsuit, towels

4. Practice tapes and tape recorder

5. Food items to supplement meals such as fruit, granola bars, juice, etc.

6. Fun items such as team mascots

7. Money or travelers' checks

8. Copy of the practice schedule if applicable

Coach's Checklist for the Trip

1. Music and equipment (tapes, tape recorder, adapters, etc.)

2. Official USSS Handbook (rulebook) and Guidelines

3. Copy of the meet flier

4. Rooming list for the hotel

5. Hotel confirmation (may be the responsibility of the chaperone)

6. Team banner (may be assigned to the chaperone or a swimmer)

7. Emergency medical forms

Team Rules

Knowing team rules also contributes to a successful trip; do not hesitate to hand out a list of rules and regulations. When planning a long trip, encourage swimmers to bring along some items to amuse themselves with, such as cards and crossword puzzles.

Tell the swimmers that they are expected to behave in a well-mannered, orderly fashion throughout the trip. In the hotel, there should be no running around or loud yelling. They must respect the property of others and observe bedtime curfews. Good pool manners require that the swimmers line up quietly for figures, keep the locker rooms clean (including cleaning up the unflavored gelatin used in their hair) and applaud all competitors.

Chaperones

If your organization uses chaperones, take time to meet with the parents to determine the chaperone's responsibilities. A good chaperone can be the key to a successful trip. This person may have the following responsibilities:

1. Checking the team into the hotel.

2. After checking with the coach, getting the swimmers to the pool on time.

3. Seeing that the swimmers eat well.

4. Supervising bedtime curfews.

5. Arranging sightseeing excursions with the permission of the coach.

Fund Raising

Fund raising is a topic of paramount interest to all coaches. A team needs a major financial plan for the year that includes ample opportunities for team members to raise sufficient money for travel. As a team progresses to higher levels of competition, the plan must become more ambitious and may require separate fund-raising committees. Bake sales, flower sales, candy sales, raffles, swim-a-thons, water shows, and demonstrations are all methods that can generate needed funds.

Medical Forms

Each team member's parents should fill out an emergency medical form that the coach brings to swim meets. The following form can be copied and used.

Emergency Medical Form
(Example)

My son/daughter, _____, has permission to participate in all meets, clinics, and shows involving the _____ (name of club).

Is he/she in good physical condition with no serious illness or operation since his/her last health exam?   Yes _____   No _____

Does he/she have any chronic or ongoing medical condition of which the person in charge should be aware? (Such as: allergies, diabetes, ear infections, etc.) Please specify _____
_____

Is any medication required for the above medical condition?
Yes _____   No _____   Please specify _____

Physician's Name _____ Phone _____

Parent's Medical Insurance Coverage _____Policy #_____

During these activities I may be reached at:

Address _____ Phone _____

If I am not available contact _____ Phone_____

In the event that I cannot be reached in an EMERGENCY, I hereby give permission to the physician selected by the person in charge to secure emergency treatment for my child as named above.

_____
Parent or Guardian's Signature

_____
Date

The Buddy System

The buddy system is one technique that may help swimmers on their first out-of-town meet. An older swimmer is assigned to a new swimmer to help her prepare for a couple of weeks before the trip. It is especially helpful if the more experienced swimmer/traveler is also going to the meet and can be a much needed friend and guide throughout the competition.

Epilogue

Coaching synchronized swimming can be a rewarding experience, but it is not without its share of challenges and problems. Following the guidelines in this book and in the earlier volume, *Coaching Synchronized Swimming Effectively*, will certainly help you meet those challenges and solve some of the problems you encounter. A synchro coach has no greater satisfaction than that of viewing a team or trio of swimmers she has taught and nurtured. The smiles on their faces, their hair neatly tucked under a beautifully designed, water-proof sequined hat, and the synchronicity of movements you have taught them makes the whole process worthwhile. Do not wait for the next book. Get out to the pool and coach. Synchro wants you. Good luck!

Bibliography

Alter, J. *Surviving Exercise*. Boston: Houghton Mifflin Company.

Counsilman, J.E. (1968). *The science of swimming*. Englewood Cliffs, NJ: Prentice-Hall.

Forbes, M.S. (1984). *Coaching synchronized swimming effectively*. Champaign, IL: Human Kinetics.

Maglischo, E.W. (1982). *Swimming faster: A comprehensive guide to the science of swimming*. Palo Alto, CA: Mayfield.

Van Buskirk, K.E. (Ed.). (1985). *Official 1985-86 synchronized swimming handbook*. Indianapolis, IN: United States Synchronized Swimming, Inc.

Contributing Authors

Kaaren Babb-Kaaren Babb has been involved in synchronized swimming for 18 years. She is a national judge and the assistant coach of the long-reigning national champions, the Walnut Creek Aquanuts. Ms. Babb is currently serving synchro as a consultant to the U.S. National Training Squad, as Chairperson of the Age Group Committee, as the West Zone Chairperson, and as the mother of two national training squad members.

Dawn Bean-Dawn Bean has a BA in physical education from the University of California at Berkeley. Her involvement in synchro spans 46 years. She currently is the President of Synchro-USA and has served as a representative to the U.S. Olympic Committee Executive Board and House of Delegates. She is an international judge, a noted worldwide speaker at seminars and clinics, and the editor/publisher of *Synchro* magazine. Her honors include the Lillian MacKellar Distinguished Service Award and induction into the Hall of Fame.

Ross Bean-Ross Bean, who holds a PhD in biochemistry from the University of California at Berkeley, has been involved in synchro for 35 years. He currently serves as an international judge and Chairperson of the Figures

Committee, and is the author of numerous articles and figure analyses for *Synchro* magazine. He is also a Hall of Famer and recipient of the Lillian MacKellar Distinguished Service Award.

Christine Carver-Chris Carver is the head coach of the Santa Clara Aquamaids. In her work with this strong California club, Ms. Carver has produced several national champions and national training squad members, as well as international age group champions. She serves as a national judge and has been head coach of the Classical Splash touring team.

Charlotte Davis-Charlotte Davis earned a BA in speech and secondary education from the University of Washington. Highlights of her 23 years in synchronized swimming include being named an All American athlete in 1970 and USSS Coach of the Year in 1983 and serving as the 1984 Olympic coach. She currently is the head coach of the U.S. National Training Squad and serves as a national judge.

EmmaGene Edwards-EmmaGene Edwards earned a BS in health and physical education from James Madison University. She has served for 18 years as a coach and judge in the Florida Gold Coast area and as a national judge. She is also an Instructor-Trainer for the USSS Coaching Certification Program.

Pam Edwards-Pam Edwards has been involved in synchro as both an athlete and a coach for 28 years. She received numerous national and international awards as an athlete in the late 1960s and has since coached others to national and international finalist positions. She is an assistant coach for the Walnut Creek Aquanuts and also serves as the National Team I manager, as the Chairperson of the Athletes Training Committee, and as a member of the Figures Committee.

Gail Emery-Gail Emery received a BS in recreation from California State University at Hayward. During her 25-year involvement in synchro, she was a national and international champion and All American athlete in the late 1960s and was named coach of the Year in 1984, 1985, and 1986. She is the head coach of the seven-time defending national champion Walnut Creek Aquanuts and is the assistant coach of the National Training Squad. Gail served as the 1984 Olympic Team Manager and is a national judge. Her accomplishments earned her the Hall of Fame award in 1985.

Margaret Swan Forbes-Margaret Forbes holds an MS in physical education from Trinity University. Her synchro involvement spans 30 years. She is an international judge and also conducts clinics. She authored the *Coaching Synchronized Swimming Effectively* teaching manual. The manager of the 1971 Pan American Games, Ms. Forbes received the Hall of Fame and the San Antonio Sportswoman of the Year Awards.

Avilee Goodwin-Avilee Goodwin has a BA in dance and an MA in animated film from San Francisco State University. A former senior and junior national solo, duet, and team finalist, Ms. Goodwin coached for a couple of years before retiring from synchro after 11 years to concentrate on dance. She is the founder of Moving Basis, a modern dance company based in San Francisco. She provided the illustrations in this manual.

Peg Hogan-Peg Hogan earned an MA in physical education from the University of Maryland. Her 27 years in synchro have been spent in nearly all aspects of the sport—as a master's athlete, as a national judge, and as a coach at the age group and intercollegiate levels. She is the Chairperson of Judges Training and was the 1980 Master Swimmer of the Year. She was one of only two swimmers to receive three gold medals at the 1985 World Masters Games.

Virginia Jasontek-Ginny Jasontek received an MA in education from Xavier University. During her 30 years in synchro, she has served as a national and international judge, coached Ohio's senior champions and senior national finalists, and was the Vice-President of Officials on the USSS Board of Directors. She was named greater Cincinnati's Coach of the Year in 1980 and was the 1984 recipient of the Lillian MacKellar Distinguished Service Award.

Kathy Kretschmer-Huss-Kathy Kretschmer-Huss has been in synchro for 25 years, as both an athlete and a coach. As a swimmer, she was an international solo and national solo and duet champion, a Pan American team champion, and a recipient of the 1976 Hall of Fame award. She coached the 1981 and 1984 Intercollegiate National Champions and was a National Training Squad assistant coach. She is currently a national judge.

Linda Lichter-Linda Lichter has a BS in physical education from Southern Connecticut State University. During her 20 years in synchro, she has been a national judge and an assistant coach to the National Training Squad. She coached a team to second place in the senior national championships and is currently coaching an age group team.

Lillian MacKellar-Billie MacKellar is a past Chairman (President) of United States Synchronized Swimming and serves on the USSS Board of Directors. Her involvement in synchro spans more than 40 years, during which time she produced national solo and duet champions. She has traveled all over the world lecturing and teaching synchro at clinics and seminars. She is the first recipient of the award that bears her name, the Lillian MacKellar Distinguished Service Award. She is also a Hall of Fame inductee and a renowned international judge.

Gail Pucci-Gail Pucci has been involved in synchro as an athlete, coach, and judge for 22 years. As an athlete, she was the 1973 World Duet and Team Champion, the 1975 World and Pan American Solo and Team Champion, and a 1975 Hall of Fame award recipient. Ms. Pucci coached the world champion team in 1978, was again named to the Hall of Fame in 1979, and was an assistant coach of the National Training Squad. She is currently an assistant coach of the defending national champions.

Dorothy Sowers-Dottie Sowers, who received a BS in physical education from the State University of New York at Cortland, has been involved in synchro for 36 years. During that time, she has coached a senior national finalist team, and served as a national judge and the Chairperson of the National Judges Testing Committee. She was the

1980 Lillian MacKellar Distinguished Service Award recipient and a 1981 Hall of Fame inductee.

Joanmarie Vanaski-Joanmarie Vanaski has served in synchro in many capacities— as an athlete, coach and judge and as a consultant to the National Training Squad. She swam at Ohio State University on an athletic scholarship before retiring to coach. She currently works as a dance specialist in the Contra Costa area.

Kim E. Van Buskirk-Kim Van Buskirk holds an MS in athletic administration from Western Illinois University and is working on a PhD in sport psychology from Ohio State University. During her 20 years in synchro, she has been a national caliber athlete, a coach, and a national judge. She was honored in 1985 as a United States Information Agency Sport Diplomat to Uruguay and Argentina. Kim served as the Director of Educational Services for USSS from 1983-1986. During her tenure with the USSS she conducted clinics throughout the United States, coordinated the national camp program, and oversaw the Coaching Certification Program. Ms. Van Buskirk is the Deputy Commissioner for Synchronized Swimming at the tenth Pan American Games to be held in Indianapolis, Indiana, in 1987.

Joanne Wright-Joanne Wright received her AA in recreation supervision from Erie Community College. Her synchro involvement spans 22 years and includes participation as a national judge and as the head choreographer and assistant coach of a senior national finalist team.

Index